THE INNER JURY

the INNER JURY

WINNING TRIALS WITH

STRATEGIC PSYCHOLOGY
MODERN TRIAL SCIENCE
SOLUTIONS TO COMMON DILEMMAS

BRUCE B. WHITMAN

Pine Street Press

THE INNER JURY

WINNING TRIALS BY STRATEGIC PSYCHOLOGY, MODERN TRIAL SCIENCE, SOLUTIONS TO COMMON DILEMMAS

Published by:
Pine Street Press, LLC

Printed in the United States of America

ISBN-13: 978-0-9882052-3-9
ISBN-10: 0988205238

Edited by: Julia Kantor
Book layout by: Adina Cucicov, Flamingo Designs

This book is dedicated to my loving wife and fellow trial lawyer Ginny, my two dynamic sons, Jake and Andrew, the memory of my warm and fun loving mother, Dorothy Yarbrough, my father, the insightful Freudian analyst, Dr. Roy Whitman, my brothers and sisters and extended family and friends.

Stuart and Mary Kay,
Hope you enjoy the book.
Read it before bed for maximum sleep.
Bruce

Contents

Introduction

One jury in the California desert comes back with a $16 million verdict in a case with questionable causation. Another jury in Chicago arrives at a "Christmas present" verdict of $17 million in a cerebral palsy birth injury case. Yet, across the country, numerous other juries routinely decide that the injured party should get nothing or clearly less than is fair. Defendants are often given a "pass" for conduct that is negligent, but not grossly negligent.

Is this jury nullification?[1] Are juries rebelling against the system of fault?

Why does one jury come back into the courtroom with a verdict for the injured party, but so many others do not? Why do over 85% of medical malpractice trials in many jurisdictions reportedly result in a defense verdict? Are the plaintiff lawyers taking on frivolous cases, even though it is financially foolish to do so?[2] It seems unlikely, but salmon do keep swimming upriver and lemmings follow each other over cliffs to their death.

Can it be that trial lawyers are often wrong in evaluating cases? Or, should we look at other factors and admit that lawyers representing the plaintiffs are missing some important elements that have not been widely addressed?

---

1 Jury nullification occurs when the jury understands but simply refuses to follow the law as instructed by the judge because of shared psychosocial or political reasons.

2 Since attorney fees in most tort cases are based on contingency, if there is a defense verdict, the injured party and the lawyer get nothing. Furthermore, because the cost of taking a civil case through trial is typically covered as an advance by the lawyer, he or she will usually lose money, often a large sum into six figures, in case of a defense verdict.

The thesis of this book is that most cases are not frivolous and defense lawyers are not innately better or better trained than plaintiff lawyers. Rather, there are structural and emotional barriers that jurors face before awarding damages in a trial, *even when, objectively, liability has been established.* So, lawyers cannot assume that a full compensatory assessment of damages by the jury, or even a favorable verdict, will logically follow from what the lawyers consider a strong case.

Resistance to awarding damages is deep and in the unconscious part of the brain. Lawyers must find ways to overcome such deep barriers in order to win trials and achieve success for their clients. Over time, to help jurors overcome resistance and other barriers, many very smart and dedicated trial lawyers and consultants have addressed this seminal problem with a variety of scientific methods of jury selection, evidence presentation strategies, and ways of framing arguments. However, the dynamic psychology of a jury is too often overlooked.

Some barriers are the result of intentional conservative control of legal institutions and committees who write the pattern jury instructions that most judges use. For example, virtually all courts place the "burden of proof" on the plaintiff side and set up high bars for what must be proven to overcome that burden. These "institutional" barriers can be argued to the court or the jury as unfair or picked apart in the final argument.

The most critical barrier, however—as I have learned in my 30 years in court—is unconscious resistance by the jury. This is what I call the "Peter and Paul" problem—the fact that in order for the plaintiff to be awarded compensatory damages for injury, the jury must take money from the defendant to give to the plaintiff.

Our forefathers included in our Constitution the right to a jury. In Ohio, where I have mainly practiced, this right is "inviolate."[3] But, as Michelle Alexander, author of the bestseller "The New Jim Crow," recently wrote in The New York Times, constitutional rights to a jury trial and to confront witnesses for criminal defendants have become "theoretical," as prosecutors are now allowed to threaten much longer incarceration if there is a jury conviction. This has largely created a system of plea bargaining.

3 Ohio Constitution, Article I, Section 10.

Increasingly, the same holds true in civil cases. As trial lawyers, we must counsel our clients that a jury may provide nothing for an injured person or fired employee. Jurors are not cold and callous by nature, but modern jury instructions are confusing, ambiguous, and tend to protect the negligent persons, rather than the victim. As a result, even when a jury does award damages in a negligence case, the amount is often considerably less than what is necessary to reimburse the injured person for all losses, including the cost of litigation.

Jurors must feel that they are doing the right thing. To facilitate that, we must create a psychodynamic courtroom, where the jurors' unconscious need to be empathetic to the victim is encouraged and nurtured, notwithstanding the forces against such altruism.

Juries are only acting humanly when they protect someone who has made a "legal mistake" without intentional misconduct. There does not seem to be a groundswell for imminent change of this system of burden, so the only answer is to overcome jurors' conscious resistance to change the status quo by eliciting their unconscious desire to help the one who has been harmed.[4]

Trial lawyers have a variety of modern resources to help them produce persuasive evidence of both liability and damages. Still, it is hard to get juries to take money from the "nice," but negligent, defendants.[5] Remember, the redistribution of wealth by government force[6] to solve inequality is probably the most divisive political issue in our society today. Dealing with this on an unconscious and emotional level is difficult for most people. Success at trial may depend on how well we can separate

---

4 The other problem, of course, is that most jurisdictions don't allow the jury to be informed that there is an insurance or self-insurance plan that would actually pay the damages. Some jurors might derive comfort in knowing for sure that the money would not be coming directly out of a "nice" defendant's pocket.

5 More than 50 years ago, Berkeley law professor Albert Eherzweig postulated that the "Fault Rule" of negligence law would ultimately fail, as it is inconsistent with Freudian principles of the unconscious. "A Psychoanalysis of Negligence," Northwestern University Law Review, 47, 855-872, 1953.

6 We must also remember that the courts are the third branch of government in the mind of a juror. To a juror, who is summoned to serve, the court is acting as the government when a verdict is reached.

our case from the sociopolitical battle, so that even a conservative could feel comfortable voting for compensatory damages.

Of course, we can try to demonize the defendants in the traditional manner. In my experience, however, demonizing only works when the tortfeasor is noticeably rude or unlikeable. A lawyer is not often so lucky.

There are many gentler ways to overcome this unconscious barrier. By applying various psychodynamic methods, tried and true outside of the courtroom, we can make the jury feel that they are doing right to compensate a victim, even if doing so may be contrary to some of their sociopolitical philosophies.

I believe those representing the plaintiffs have underestimated the difficulty jurors must face in that last step of deliberation and decision. By using psychodynamic methods to mine the depths of the unconscious, we can persuade the jury that it is okay to make an exception to the most basic of all rules in our society: "My property is my property, Peter's property is Peter's, and I cannot decide to give Peter's property to Paul—only Peter can do that." First, however, we must understand how the conscious and unconscious sides of the human mind work and influence each other.

Here are the key questions I will try to answer in this book:

1. Why do some lawyers succeed and others fail to convince juries to award a verdict not just for the plaintiff, but *against the defendant*?

2. How can we mine the unconscious to reach jurors so they can feel that compensation is a good thing, *even though it is a forced redistribution of wealth*?

3. How can we understand better what we need to do to create a silent, secondary dialogue with the jury, anticipating and answering their questions and supplying the information in a way that helps them overcome deeply ingrained barriers?

As with any endeavor, we must start with ourselves. First, we have to understand some basic principles about the unconscious, so that we can address the unconscious resistance of the jurors. Second, we have to brush up on the latest research by trial consultants and modern scholar-lawyers, learning the skills and methods necessary to increase our persuasive abilities to influence the unconscious. Third, we have to acknowledge openly and transparently in court that our legal system arms juries with potential to do something that contrasts the basic "Peter and Paul" principle of our society, which may be unthinkable in most other circumstances. Finally, we can look to other specialties, such as medicine or sports, to find new methods that could be translated to law.

The first skill of a trial lawyer is not brilliant oration or cross-examination; it is being a great *listener*. We have to listen to our clients, to our experts, and to people's opinions about what we do, as well as to skepticism and cynicism about our tort law system. Afterward, we also need to *acknowledge* that this skepticism exists. Furthermore, as unfair as we may perceive it to be, we must refrain from battling the societal bias against us, choosing instead to work within it. Finally, we need to develop our psychodynamic skills, as well as our trial skills, so that we can *influence* and even change how jurors think.

Prior to all of this, however, we must *believe*. If we want jurors to believe, we ourselves have to believe. A trial lawyer must be an optimist and have faith in the innate goodness of mankind and its ability to solve problems in an ethical and altruistic way. We must believe that deep resistance is largely one that we can overcome. This inner belief is the first and the most essential step toward reaching jurors and *persuading* them to feel empathy.

The main teaching of this book is how to psychodynamically use unconscious communication in the courtroom (or the mediation room) through spoken and unspoken phenomena of *transference, hinting, projecting, framing, polarizing,* and other techniques to influence the unconscious thinking of a jury. The goal is to create a gut feeling that our case is right and the other side's defense is not, enabling the jury to develop a shared *intuitive* sense that, based on all of the cues received at the trial, they should demand sufficient amount of money *from the damaging party* to help the harmed person have a better life.

We are asking the jurors to create an *entitlement* for our clients and their families. We have to acknowledge this up front and then go to work on convincing the jury that this is the right thing to do. Modern theorists in psychology believe it is best to work *with*, rather than against, resistance, as resistance leads the way to a deeper layer of self-awareness. We need to pattern our work in the courtroom in this way as well, finding resistance in voir dire and then working with it throughout the trial to eventually overcome it.

Early scholars of the human mind, like Freud and Jung, have given us the foundation for such persuasion. In this book, I will show you how my own trials, as well as those of other lawyers, have either benefited or suffered from the unconscious communication between attorney and jury.

While I can only touch upon the huge body of knowledge about the human mind and its relevance to jury trials, I believe that each of us must learn how the unconscious works and how we can get over the natural resistance to change in the courtroom and beyond. Knowing how to use modern trial methods and skills in conjunction with these psychodynamic methods is bound to bring greater success for us and our clients.

PART I

The Psychodynamic Courtroom

Chapter 1

The "Peter and Paul" Problem

There has been a huge amount of thought, research, and trial lawyers' and consultants' personal anecdotes published to address how to approach juries and what is important in jury trials. Most of this literature concentrates on strategies and approaches of how the lawyer should prepare, what the lawyer should say, and how he or she should present the case. This is all certainly important, but what has been largely ignored is seeing the case from every perspective, including the viewpoint of the juror, individually and as part of a group.

We must remember that jurors know nothing about the case or the people involved when they first sit down. They then gradually learn about the case passively through listening. At the end, though, the process of passive listening suddenly ceases, leaving the jury to make a decision by themselves—with little outside help, other than obtuse and ambiguous jury instructions.

The first thing a lawyer must do when entering trial is gain awareness of what the trial offers for and asks of *the jury*, not the client. This is easier said than done, since all of the preparation we do to get the case to court is focused on what the trial will be about for our client. The jury's role is to decide who will win and what will happen monetarily. So, we have to get our minds around the variances of *getting*, which is what our client wants, *giving*, which we want the jury to do, and *taking*, which the jury has to do in order to give.

If we could tell the jury that the court has an unlimited pot of money, that each of the parties starts at zero, and that the jury has the power to make an accounting decision to *give* the injured person compensation for injuries, the injured person would undoubtedly win virtually every trial, *getting* bills paid and additional money for pain and suffering. If people are on the whole altruistic, the dismal rate of success for injured persons in jury trials must be from other causes.

The unrecognized reality for lawyers is that jurors are also looking at the *taking* part in equal measure. As altruistic as they may have been at the outset, at the end of the trial they are told that whatever they give will come not from some neutral pot, but from the pocket of the defendant.

This is a dilemma for plaintiff lawyers because it can make us look greedy, vindictive, and insensitive in the jury's eyes, even though we try to portray ourselves as positive, altruistic, and caring. Worse, this "taking dilemma" is something that jurors only come to fully realize at the end of the trial, when instructed by the court that they must decide not only in favor of the injured person, but also against the other party.

In the minds of the jurors, they can simply maintain the status quo by a defense verdict, leaving the situation financially the same as before the proceedings. Psychologically, jurors may find this a lot easier to live with than being a tool by which the court (the government, in the eyes of the jury) takes money from one person to give to another. This "Paul and Peter" problem is a predominant reason that trials are unexpectedly lost when everything "seemed to be going so well."

Understanding the jury's dilemma is the first step to overcoming this challenge. By using psychodynamics, opening ourselves to the jury, to delve deep into the unconscious of the jurors, we can help them resolve their resistance to taking. Psychotherapeutic tools, those actually deployed in the field of psychology in patient care, can further enable us to effectively persuade the jury to feel satisfied about taking, as well as giving.

Chapter 2

Positivity—
The Essential Psychodynamic Tool

How can we as lawyers use psychotherapeutic methods and principles in the courtroom to persuade a jury to overcome deep unconscious resistance to take from Peter to compensate Paul? Or, how could defense lawyers use them to defeat a plaintiff who is profoundly and visibly injured, apparently by the accident at issue?[7]

We do not all have the western drawl of Gerry Spence or the southern charm of Don Keenan. But, all of us can, in our own unique ways, be a positive force in the courtroom. The first psychodynamic tool for dealing with the dilemma of juror resistance is *positivity*[8, 9]—positivity toward the jury, the witnesses, the courtroom staff, the media, and, most of all, our client.

My first lesson in positivity as an effective psychodynamic tool for trial lawyers in the courtroom took place well before I became a lawyer.

When I was 16, many years ago, my mother plowed her boat into a barge on the Ohio River. When I got to the hospital, I saw my mother's flawless face battered and lacerated, her cheekbones busted up so badly that the surgeon had to wire the chips of the cheekbone together. I was shocked and scared.

---

7 In this book, I will usually focus on the plaintiff lawyer because that is what I do, but similar psychodynamic solutions can be used by defense counsel to solve their dilemmas.

8 Carl Rogers, psychologist and scholar, wrote extensively that therapists trying to create a therapeutic alliance with a patient should always approach the patient with "unconditional positive regard."

9 Norman Vincent Peale wrote the "Power of Positive Thinking" in 1952. Since then, the book has reportedly sold over 7 million copies.

I had just recently passed the driving test and received my driver's license. When I left the hospital, still upset, I made an illegal left turn and ran into another car. The accident was my fault. The other driver claimed he had suffered whiplash and a back injury and sued.

Five years later, the case went to a jury trial. My mother and I sat together at the table with our lawyer. The other driver was brought into the courtroom dressed in a prisoner uniform; he was doing time for some minor assault or theft. At the beginning of the trial, I was sure we would win, even though I knew I had caused the accident. Surely a jury wouldn't take our money and give it to a criminal!

The plaintiff lawyer was an energetic, flamboyant, and charismatic young man with an earring. He was cheerful and positive about *everything.* He asked the jury if they could be fair to his client. He joked with them and poked fun at himself, his earring, and even his client's jailhouse rags.

I can't remember any of the specific voir dire of the jury, but I do remember him discussing the fact that his client was in jail for an unrelated matter. I can't remember any of the specific questions to witnesses, but I vividly recall him being positive and optimistic in the final argument, highlighting how the money would help his client.

My lawyer was a square, non-descript insurance lawyer, selected and paid for by our car insurer. He was not positive in any way. He just seemed bored. We lost the trial.

I learned then, as a defendant, that the positivity of a lawyer has an unconscious effect on the jury, even though I didn't understand the psychodynamic reasons behind this phenomenon at the time. I could simply *feel* the jury relate positively to the plaintiff lawyer as he walked around the courtroom. His very movements were positive, and he seemed completely at ease.

What unconscious, unspoken forces inhabited that courtroom? The plaintiff lawyer appeared the embodiment of a good son, a fun brother, and a young active father. With this positive image firmly embedded in the unconscious of the jury, I believe he enabled the jurors to "open up" to his side of the argument. Through his positive approach, he also helped them overcome the difficult dilemma of taking money from a "nice" family like my mother and me, convincing the jury to award this money to a plaintiff in jailhouse clothes.

How can we put a positive message on *taking* from a "nice" defendant who made a careless mistake without malice? Why not say something like this right at the beginning of voir dire, as positively and transparently as possible?

"Ladies and gentlemen, we as lawyers have a duty to ask you, the jury, to do very unusual things. For example, if it is the right thing to do by law, can you take this doctor's money and give it to this patient?"

Or,

"Can you accept that it is a good thing to award a verdict to Mr. I., knowing that the money to pay the verdict will not come from the court, but from Dr. N?"

It is important to approach the jury positively with this proposition. It is also important to positively support the *taking* part of their decision throughout the trial.

If it is comfortable, you can propose the following questions to the opposing witnesses, experts, and even the defendant:

"Sir, if in fact, by law, Dr. N's negligence did cause this harm and injury, you would have no problem with the concept that he should pay, would you?"

And,

"Sir, this is a good thing that our law system provides—do you agree?"

Positivity does not mean we should ignore problems in our case or legal issues that may be difficult for jurors to understand. On the contrary, it prompts us to admit the dilemma we are about to thrust upon the jury. We should discuss openly the difficulty the jury may have in finding that the defendant will have to pay. Furthermore, we need to address the issue positively, as a way to even things up. We must present it as a good thing that is not vindictive or coercive, but an opportunity for everyone to do the right thing.

Remember, positivity does not equal bravado, nor does it preclude a healthy dose of self-deprecation or conceding certain facts that might not be perfect in your case. However, make sure you never concede anything that is central to the case.

While it is important to emphasize that the law allows the jury to favor the plaintiff direction, in these days of anti-lawyer advertising and tort reform, it is no longer sufficient to show that our client has been injured and is entitled to damages as a result. As the trial moves ahead, we have to do more—we have to use positivity to persuade the jury that it is OK, from the sociopolitical perspective, to demand the person causing the injury to pay an injured party. How? By asking the witnesses to agree that the system is fair, that the law is good, and that if they were in the shoes of the plaintiff, they would sue for damages, too. By doing so, we will allow the jurors to overcome this long-standing "Peter and Paul" dilemma.

Chapter 3

Negligence and Psychotherapeutic Tools

In any trial, the injured person's lawyer has to prove to the jury, at the very least, that the perpetrator was negligent. What is "negligent"? In most places, the court will instruct the jury that negligence is the failure to use "ordinary care," or care that a reasonably careful person would use under the same or similar circumstances.

This is not the way people normally talk when discussing how an accident or injury might have happened. Making a case of negligence is, therefore, a primary dilemma for the trial lawyer, as the definition of negligence is bound to be unfamiliar and confusing to the jury. What is "ordinary"? Who is a "reasonably careful person"? Doesn't a reasonably careful person make mistakes? Mistakes are forgiven, aren't they?

In many cases, lawyers feel it is necessary to hire so-called "experts" to explain why the careless person should be held liable. Meanwhile, the other side hires counter-experts to explain why the accident occurred despite the person being careful; this "s*** happens" defense often works very well.

How does a jury typically think about this nebulous concept of "negligence"? Most jurors will likely think of "negligence" as synonymous with "mistake." We can read definitions, jury instructions, and explain negligence to jurors, but because mistakes are often excusable outside the courtroom, most jurors, in their unconscious minds, will have a high level of resistance to making a person pay money for a mistake.

The notion that it is human to err is deeply imbedded in our culture. So, we have to either prove that much more than a mistake took place or convince the jury that this mistake was a negligent one. But, how do we overcome the jury's resistance to punishing those who are only human?

There is an entire industry of lawyers and trial consultants who make a very good living teaching trial tactics to aspiring lawyers on this very topic: how to dress, where to stand, how to select the best jurors, how to demonize the defendant, and how to polarize the case. These are all valuable and necessary strategies that every trial lawyer has to learn before stepping into the courtroom. However, lawyers also need to dive deeper into the way jurors think, the dilemmas they face in their unique role, and the confusion they are likely to feel over the legal lingo that only lawyers can clear up.

Confusion inherently causes resistance. In their efforts to provide clarity to confusing concepts and thereby overcome resistance, lawyers need to look to psychology.

The genesis of psychodynamic solutions to unconscious resistance can be traced to the development of psychology, psychiatry, and psychotherapy. A century ago, a group of researchers in the embattled profession of psychiatry searched for a way to help patients with mental disorders get better and live normal lives with their families, rather than suffer in agony and deep emotional pain. The core idea, advanced by Sigmund Freud and then adapted by Carl Gustav Jung and many others, was that a therapist, by uncovering how the unconscious brain worked, could help a patient get better by allowing the patient to gain insight.

There are core psychotherapeutic tools that therapists use to help patients delve deeply into their unconscious. These include transference, unconditional positive regard, free association, dream analysis, and even hypnosis, among others. Lawyers can use some of the same methods, in modified ways, to provide clarity and allow jurors to gain insight.

Following the steps of pioneers like Freud, Jung, Carl Rogers, Erik Erikson, Wilfred Bion, Kay Jamison, and Glen Gabbard, modern psychologists such as Daniel Kahnemann and Gary Klein have dedicated their lives to researching the psychodynamic tools we need to tap into the unconscious of not only patients, but students, employees, and groups as well. Creation and careful nurturing of the therapeutic alliance, transference, countertransference, established boundaries, and intuition can help us overcome juror resistance in the same way that these tools help patients heal and lead productive lives.

The juror, much like the patient, is often internally confused and looking for clarity. Through these psychodynamic solutions, we can guide jurors toward insight and influence how they unconsciously engage in intuitive thinking, empathy, and decision-making.

To be most effective, we need to merge psychodynamic solutions with the more traditional methods of information delivery outlined by legal scholars like David Ball, Don Keenan, Rick Friedman, and Gerry Spence. This will allow the information we present to be better received by jurors at the unconscious and emotional level, as well as the rational and logical level. We need both to maximize our ability to influence jurors' thinking and overcome their inevitable resistance.

So, how can we adapt core psychotherapeutic methods to the courtroom? First, we can transfer our lawyerly "intuition" about the case to the jurors, so that their intuitive sense is the same as ours. In addition, we can create a trial alliance with the jury as a group, similar to the therapeutic alliance between a therapist and a patient.

As trial lawyers, we are respected for our knowledge, our competitiveness, and our success. Much like parents or older siblings, we are feared, but also idealized. Nevertheless, there is unconscious resistance to the very idea of a lawyer, which we must address each time we enter a courtroom.

Because of the partisan battle raging in our political system, the concept of frivolous lawsuits, runaway juries, and so-called "liberal" judges, many jurors have an intuitive sense that the person filing a lawsuit against someone who simply made a mistake is wrong, *no matter what the facts are*. Our duty as lawyers is to recognize this dilemma, freely acknowledge it to the jury, and then figure out ways to overcome it.

Lawyerly tactics taught in law schools through the Socratic method are not enough to deal with jurors' deep and unconscious resistance to the nebulous and confusing concepts of negligence, proximate cause, and foreseeability. Even transactional lawyers engaged in making deals or corporate mergers should study, to some degree, the unconscious mind, the way transference may cloud or clarify the receipt of information, how people are guided by intuition as well as information, and how groups make decisions. These are sophisticated and difficult concepts to learn for lawyers, as most of us pride ourselves on critical thinking, logic, and concrete decision-making, rather than esoteric principles such as intuition and projection.

Chapter 4

Jurors Speak

It is my impression from years in the courtroom that the most powerful knowledge a lawyer can have in a trial is what the jurors are thinking and how they are feeling, consciously and unconsciously. In this chapter, we will examine the thoughts of two jurors in two prominent cases across the country.

One of the jurors I interviewed, "Gail," was on a jury that returned a $16 million verdict in a medical malpractice case in California. The other juror, "Luther," who wrote a blog detailing his experience, was on a jury that returned a $17 million verdict in a childbirth medical malpractice case in Chicago.

Gail's and Luther's essentially unfiltered thoughts and memories, as presented below, show how jurors perceive trials and the lawyers involved. Moreover, they teach us how important the unconscious is in the courtroom and the jury room.

Juror Gail

It was January 2, 2009, in a county courthouse in California. The jury venire of about one hundred was led into the courtroom by the court clerk, who directed each juror to an assigned seat. Twelve were put in the jury box and the rest sent to the back of the courtroom.

Gail, juror No. 36, was seated in the third-to-last row. She worked for the city government as a clerk. She was 55 and married, with a daughter in high school. She had been on one jury years ago—for a criminal trial against a drunk driver who had lost control of the car and killed another driver. She had voted for conviction, but felt bad about it because the defendant had not intended to kill anyone.

Upon entering the courtroom this time around, Gail carefully scanned the room—her mind acting like a camera, clicking each image. Seeing an awful lot of jurors in attendance, she postulated that this must be "a big deal."

The very next thing Gail saw was a man in a wheelchair, with a woman, whom she assumed to be his wife, sitting next to him. They were nicely dressed. The wife was actively caring for the man in the wheelchair, and they were holding hands. Gail tried not to look at them. She did not want to get emotionally charged because she knew that would be unfair. She noticed several men in suits at the other table—one Asian man and two middle-aged, well-dressed, conservative-looking men. She assumed the Asian man to be the client and the other men to be his lawyers.

One of the lawyers appeared to be sick with a cold. He was sneezing and wiping his nose on his sleeve. Gail thought, "He is disgusting."

Gail continued to look around after taking a seat. The other jurors were mostly elderly. "How can I get off of this jury?" she pondered. She felt trapped. She had a lot to do in the coming weeks and just could not afford to spend weeks on a jury.

The judge entered the room. He was a good-looking, gray-haired man, dressed in robes. Once seated up on the bench, he told the jurors that the case involved medical malpractice. "Frivolous lawsuit," was the first thought in Gail's mind.

The judge announced the names of the parties, including the man and his wife. Gail heard that the Asian man was a doctor, but with "D.O.," not "M.D." She wondered what that meant.

Although she had tried not to look at the man in the wheelchair, she couldn't help herself. Upon taking another glance, she noticed that there were two lawyers there as well. They were talking in a gentle way to the man and his wife, who were still holding hands. Gail found herself feeling sympathetic to the man and his wife. At the other table, the lawyers were talking to each other and ignoring the Asian man, who was sitting at the table alone.

Gail thought there was "unity" on one side, but not on the other. Unity was a big plus to Gail.

By this time, there were a lot of "clicks" going off in her head about the case. She assumed there had been a bad injury. She respected doctors and wondered if this lawsuit was frivolous. However, she quickly dismissed that thought because of the wheelchair and the way the wife was holding the man's hand. She also had questions about the doctor, since he was not an M.D., but a D.O., and was Asian.

The first impressions of the lawyers, the parties, and the case were hard to change even as the trial moved forward, she said. Although the trial had lasted only six weeks and Gail told me her story a year later, these first impressions were still vivid in her mind.

This is especially important to consider in light of several issues of credibility that surfaced during the trial. The defense lawyers claimed that the doctor had come to the ER the night of the accident, but there was nothing he could have done to change the outcome. The man, his wife, and their friends testified that the doctor had not come in until the next day.

The ER note was dictated the next day. According to hospital rules, patients had to be seen within 20 minutes of arriving. The doctor explained that sometimes dictation was not logged into the computer system until the next day. The plaintiff attorneys called the system manager as a witness; he testified that the date was automatically inserted and the system never failed.

Gail's impression was that the doctor and his lawyers were trying to falsify the paperwork. The plaintiff lawyers were respectful to the doctor, but the defense attorneys seemed to be "disrespectful" to the man and his wife, she recalled. They were arrogant and carried themselves as though there was no way the jury could ever find for the plaintiffs.

Over the six weeks of trial, Gail felt isolated from her husband. He wanted her to tell him about the trial, but since the judge had instructed the jurors not to talk about it and Gail was "rules oriented," she would not talk to him.

Gail began to feel huge pressure during the final arguments. Both sides presented page after page of numbers, some from life care plans. No one advised the jury that they would not get the life care plans as exhibits and would have to try to remember all of the numbers. She wished the lawyers had given them one simple page of numbers for damages or at least warned them that they would not get the numbers in writing. As that hadn't happened, the jurors were forced to figure out this information on the jury interrogatories.

The jury filled out each element of damages on the jury interrogatories. The total added up to $16 million. Some of the jurors were shocked at the amount. Recalling the experience, Gail said she learned that there was a wide disparity in how people thought about money.

When I interviewed her a year later, Gail was convinced that the defense was "not finished with this yet." She was "sure" that they would appeal. She still thought about the trial, especially about the man in the wheelchair and his wife. She wondered how their life was. She thought the jury had done the right thing.

In the end, Gail told me that her initial sense of unity between the plaintiff and his wife, as well as the plaintiff and his lawyers, had resonated with the rest of the jury even as they deliberated. This unity was mirrored by the unity achieved by the jurors in the unanimous verdict.

I had thought Gail was a liberal the entire time we spoke. A few of her comments at the end of our conversation, however, caused me to ask about her political views. It turned out that she was a conservative Republican and thought the "Libs" were trying to redistribute wealth in America.

This suggests that it is not just the political preferences of the juror that control his or her willingness to compensate the injured or wronged party; the person's psychological makeup and openness to unconscious unity and family also plays a key role. This is evident from Gail's strong empathetic feelings for the couple and the sense of "family" she got from the way the plaintiff, his wife, and their lawyers showed unity. If we can create the feeling of unity, we can overcome the resistance of conservative jurors.

The lesson, therefore, is to not only find out in voir dire each juror's political views but to also make sure to ask and find out about every juror's feelings about his or her family.

Juror Luther

The juror identified as "Luther" detailed his experience of being on a jury in a multimillion medical malpractice case online. Here is his blog post, reprinted in its entirety:

Dec. 16, 2005
I Gave $17,070,000 for Christmas

My jury duty—Evelyn Araujo, seven years of age (mother Selene Araujo), versus St. Anthony Hospital and Drs. Hercule and Leong.

Impressions. Interesting trial. Unusual situation where "mom" (the legal term used by lawyers) had a grand mal seizure during labor, not of the eclampsic type (sort of an uncommon pregnancy type thing characterized mainly by high blood pressure, we learned). Mom had a minor history of seizures as a child.

Nurse Garcia called the resident, Dr. Wang (female), who called the on-call emergency obstetrician, Dr. Jaques Hercule, the voodoo doctor from Haiti, who ordered Valium for the seizure, had mom moved to the OR for a possible emergency C-section, etc., all in accordance with what they call the "standard of care."

After a seizure, it is expected that "baby" (as the lawyers refer to baby) would go into bradycardia, or low heart rate, as seen on the fetal monitor strip, which results in hypoxia, or oxygen deprivation. Sometimes this does not change, as when the placenta detaches from the uterine wall, but in this case the heart rate was rising, mom being intubated in the OR, and slowly came up to normal over a period of about 20 minutes.

So the question was: Should Dr. Hercule have done a crash C-section and tried to resuscitate baby outside the womb, or did his choice of natural placental resuscitation produce the cerebral palsy baby? The regular attending physician, Dr. Leong, arrived about 30 minutes after the seizure and performed an emergency C-section.

We heard from heavyweight experts, pro and con. Dr. Schrifin, the father of fetal monitoring, who has analyzed 250,000 fetal monitoring strips. Dr. David Naidich, the father and guru of pediatric neuroradiology, and the greediest whore at $700/hour. Professors, neonatologists, maternal fetal medicine specialists, pediatric neurologists, geneticists.

By the time we got into the jury room, we were all a little pissed off that we had been getting $17.20/day for the last three weeks and expert witnesses had been making $30,000 and more, so we just flipped a coin and started throwing out millions like they were nickels. (Just kidding.)

First I reported to the Daley Center, Room 1700, and got a panel number. My panel of 36 was sent to Judge Donald Devlin's courtroom, where numerous lawyers, plaintiff, and secondary defendant, Dr. Leong, were introduced to us. Surprisingly, the judge did most of the questioning, following the questionnaire potential jurors are required to make out, except for the section about any experiences in criminal court.

I had been called previously in Rolling Meadows to jury duty and was sort of expecting questioning on experience in criminal court, so I could bring up my three felony trials and get out of jury duty. No such luck. I suppose if potential jurors in Chicago were questioned on their experiences in criminal court, there would be no black jurors on juries.

Plaintiff's mother had been born in Mexico, and one potential juror boldly asked if these people were illegal aliens. The judge admonished him, of course. I wished I had been so bold. This guy wasn't picked, of course. The judge allowed little questioning by the lawyers on voir dire. At the end of the first day, I was one of eight jurors picked. Didn't really bother me much, actually, as the Daley Center is convenient and I just work on weekends. The next day four more and two alternates were picked. Sigh. Turned out to be a three-week trial.

My impressions of the trial. I was surprised at the quality of the lawyers and witnesses. See the Web page I made up. It is not complete, since we were not allowed to take notes home and my memory is fading, but illustrative.

The primary trial lawyers, Mark Clore from Texas for the plaintiff and David Hall for the defense, were certainly a step above my old lawyers Julius Lucius Echeles and Allen Masters, who have, I believe, five felony convictions between them. I don't have a picture of Clore on my Web page, but he was a dark-haired, stocky fellow, perhaps a Texas high school fullback, I imagined.

David Hall represented the hospital and Dr. Hercule, and the other defendant, Dr. Leong, was flanked by his own two lawyers, Brian Rocca and his assistant. I wish I had a picture of her, since she had the most beautiful, dramatic Spanish eyes I have [ever] seen, but a description would not do her justice. Hall had a great-looking assistant also. The hospital also had a female lawyer there, but Clore and Hall did most of the "lawyering." One of my first conclusions was that to be a good trial lawyer, you should have a resonant voice.

I preferred Hall as a lawyer, finding Clore a bit manipulative, playing the jury, and sometimes overly abrasive, but the other 11 preferred Clore. Hall was pretty straightforward, presenting his case and not being combative with witnesses.

There were quite a few witnesses. I hadn't realized there were so many specialties and sub-specialties. I hadn't heard of neonatologists and MFMs (maternal fetal medicine specialists) before. Perhaps this will sound stupid, but before having exhibits placed before me for study, I hadn't realized that babies hung upside down in mommies like vampire bats!

Most of the witnesses cancelled out from opposition testimony on lack of great relevance. It was somewhat disgusting, as well as amusing, to hear how much the expert witnesses were being paid, generally $400-700/hour. One fellow testified he was paid about $30,000 to testify. I don't know why he was asked to total his pay; he was the only one so questioned.

All [of] the expert witnesses sounded fantastic, until the lawyers got to the part about how much they were being paid Ha, ha. They, in general, were not without some shame, as the question obviously elicited some degree of discomfort. It wasn't easy for us jurors to listen to either, as we were being paid $17.20/day. I was surprised that even the anesthesiologist in the case was paid for his testimony, since he was testifying as an ordinary witness, not an expert.

I thought the case hinged on the testimony of Dr. Naidich. He gave a very long lecture on the brain (left hemisphere, right hemisphere, putamen, basal ganglia, blah, blah) and gave the opinion that Evelyn's brain damage was specific to an "acute hypoxic ischemic event" (i.e., lack of oxygen to the brain). His specialty is pediatric neuroradiology, and his analysis of MRIs was unrebutted. He was a very impressive witness, lectured like a full professor—albeit somewhat cozy with plaintiff's lawyer and well paid at $700/hour—very convincing.

Rather amusing, when introduced by Mr. Clore and asked if he had ever acted as president of the Society of Pediatric Neuroradiology (I think I got that right), he said he had, and when asked how this came about, he responded that he was the founder of the society. Other doctors during the course of the trial referred to Dr. Naidich as a "legend," so he was no doubt a real heavyweight witness.

Interestingly, he was able to point out things on the screen used for visuals using a laser pointer with almost no quivering of the laser spot on the screen. A real steady hand there, which I found unusual. One might think a man of his age would have a few tremors in the hand, compared to the younger lawyers who made much use of the laser pointer.

Another weighty factor was that Dr. Hercule simply left the OR when the regular obstetrician showed up, without so much as a how-do-you-do on how he had handled the seizure and aftermath. Dr. Leong then did an emergency C-section. I suppose the good doctors hated each other's guts, but this was not brought out in the trial. Certainly had to give such an odd performance some weight.

One would have liked to see Dr. Hercule testify in person and defend himself, but he chose to remain in Florida in his retirement, asserting that his doctor thought the travel would be too rigorous for his delicate health, and testified by videotape.

Mr. Clore made him look very bad, but I disregarded most of Clore's questioning myself, since Dr. Hercule could barely speak English and Clore's insinuating style of questioning seemed to paralyze the good doctor, like he was always expecting a trap and was reduced to shrugging his shoulders. I thought Clore's cross-examination here was a low point of the trial, but some of the other jurors took it at face value, and at face value Hercule looked like not only a jerk, but an ignorant one [as well].

The defense certainly had its share of heavyweight witnesses also. Dr. MacGregor, the top maternal fetal medicine specialist at Evanston Hospital, testified that Dr. Hercule's actions were not only proper, but preferred over a crash C-section. Certainly the seizure was well handled by all accounts, the nurse putting mom on her left side and giving oxygen, immediately calling the resident, Dr. Wang, who immediately informed Dr. Hercule, who ordered Valium for the seizure and had mom transported to the OR for a possible emergency C-section, where mom was intubated and anesthetized by Dr. Padilla.

No controversy to this point, despite the rarity of seizures. Other obstetricians testified they had never seen a seizure. The chief geneticist from Children's Memorial Hospital was another good witness for the defense.

Another problem for the plaintiff was that the American College of Obstetricians and Gynecologists had determined certain essential criteria for establishing a link between asphyxia and cerebral palsy, and Evelyn didn't really show these criteria. So, I had to go backwards to Dr. Naidich's testimony that the brain damage was specific to asphyxia and conclude that the only event in evidence that might produce asphyxia was Dr. Hercule's attentions.

In the end, the verdict was a simple legal decision—there was no deliberation except on the monetary award—but unsatisfying since one could only speculate on such things as what might have happened if Hercule had done a crash C-section, or whether Selene might have had other unattended seizures, or [whether] baby had inherited some sort of genetic disorder. And my feeling was basically, if the government has a policy of importing millions of illegal aliens from Mexico and obstetricians from Haiti, then the government should pay for the consequences.

The suing of Dr. Leong seemed a bit peculiar. Mom's labor had been progressing normally before her seizure, and thus Dr. Leong was called in from home on an emergency basis, arriving a half-hour after the seizure and having little or nothing to do with the alleged negligence and causation. Yet, he sat there patiently week after week with his two lawyers. I hope he had litigation insurance. Probably some of the easiest money his lawyer Rocca made, as he just got up now and then after the main trial lawyers were finished with witnesses and asked if anybody had any problems with Dr. Leong. Seemed like nobody did.

So why was he being sued? In his summation, Rocca blamed defense lawyer Hall for bringing up something in a deposition, but Hall wasn't doing the suing—Clore [was]. There was an issue over whether Dr. Leong or the other staffers, Dr. Wang and nurse Garcia, should have been aware of mom's history of seizures, which was available in the records, but none of the expert witnesses seemed to make much of this, perhaps because most doctors are too busy making money to bother with getting a good history.

We had one dramatic "Perry Mason" incident during the trial, and I must give credit to Mr. Clore for this. Cook County Hospital calculated fetal cord blood base deficit as -18, to the advantage of plaintiff, but a heavyweight defense doctor and researcher (Harvard, Yale, University of Chicago) recalculated the figure to be -7, to the advantage of the defense. Clore was waiting in ambush and had his textbooks, exhibits, and graphics all ready for the victim.

He started slowly, asking about how the figure was calculated, if the witness was familiar with the textbook, and if the witness would like to calculate the figure using the preferred equation from the textbook, etc. This sounds very dry, but it was dramatic to see, with the witness getting more and more uncomfortable. At the last point, plaintiff [lawyer] shot a red line across the graph on the screen to the correct figure (according to plaintiff [side]), and this was so unexpected, I gasped involuntarily.

At the end of the trial, some of the plaintiff-oriented jurors stayed to rub elbows with plaintiff. I just left, meeting the defense attorney Hall in the corridor by chance. I told him I thought he was the better lawyer, and that I thought the case was almost indeterminate. He made some comment on the poor videotaped testimony of Dr. Hercule, which could not be denied. I don't know how such a good lawyer got sandbagged by Dr. Hercule, but you make do with what you have, I suppose. He thanked me for the kind words.

As we can see from Gail's and Luther's recollections, jurors are sensitive to the symbolic family comprising the lawyer and the client. They can see the lawyer either as the unselfish father (or mother) of an intact family unit or as the detached, distant parent who doesn't really care about the family.[10] If you want to win trials, it's best to appear as the

10 Gender differences in the legal profession is a big topic. In general, I think the important thing is whether there is psychodynamic transference to a parent, not whether the transference is to a father or mother.

caring and unselfish father (or mother) figure. Jurors, like all of us, have an unconscious need to please the caring parent.

The trial lawyer must seek out opportunities to connect with jurors throughout the trial, from showing unconditional positive regard for each juror in voir dire to interacting with the client in a professional but intimate way in the view of the jury. These methods, along with some others, are similar to what therapists use to make patients feel comfortable and open.

A lawyer who shows kindness and is protective of a client can achieve a form of transference with jurors as a paternal or maternal figure, making jurors feel less resistant to the transfer of wealth from the other person to compensate the injured client.

Finally, what we have learned from Gail and Luther is that the way lawyers act is indeed very important to the jury and the way they decide the case. The lawyers who have become educated in psychotherapeutic methods of overcoming resistance and who have learned how to use these methods in the courtroom will surely have a huge advantage in the ultimate goal of persuasion. Success will follow.

Chapter 5

Transference and Countertransference

Trial lawyers need a sharper awareness of the psychodynamic theories used by psychologists and psychiatrists in therapy in order to effectively communicate with jurors. *Transference* and *countertransference* are two of the biggest concepts to learn in this regard, since both clarify and distort all human discussions and relations in the unconscious.

Transference is how the unconscious relates back to childhood experiences. *Projection* is how transference allows the unconscious mind to see a person in the present—as the emotional manifestation of the most important childhood feelings toward the mother and the father, or another important past image.

Countertransference describes how a therapist unconsciously projects a prior emotional relationship onto a patient, which often distorts the therapist's professional distance and objectivity. Countertransference can be damaging to the therapeutic goals and should be recognized and avoided or carefully managed.

I didn't learn about transference and countertransference from a book. I only learned to be aware of and use transference and projection in communicating with jurors when I represented a psychoanalyst in a case where these concepts were at issue. This experience also enabled me to realize that my presentation may be distorted by countertransference, even if I have unconsciously projected it as favorable.

Like any other new client, Dr. M had called my office and made an appointment to see me. He told me that he was a psychoanalyst, as well as a former student and colleague of my father at the department of psychiatry at a medical school. Dr. M was alleged to be a predator who was sexually abusing a patient. The doctor was in danger of losing his medical license, as well as facing criminal prosecution and a possible medical malpractice lawsuit, because he was involved in a sexual relationship with a patient. He was frightened, and after interviewing him, I knew he was right to be—he was in trouble.

I almost always represent the injured, the fired, and the criminally charged. Of course, I was also interested in taking on the case because of Dr. M's relationship with my father—and the subject matter.

The doctor told me that his sexual affair was torrid and out of control. He and his patient had been having sex in the office, at motels, and even in cars, he said. In addition, he had recently purchased a house solely for sexual trysts. His wife had no idea about the affair, but now things were dissembling. Dr. M had no difficulty understanding the legal principle of liability for a doctor having sex with a patient. He knew that he had lost control of the situation.

While the sex had been consensual initially, the patient became disillusioned and vindictive later on. She told her husband, another prominent and wealthy doctor, that Dr. M had given her powerful drugs and taken advantage of her sexually while she was in treatment. Her husband became irate and called the police. He also hired a lawyer, who subsequently wrote Dr. M a strong letter, alleging rape and threatening to sue.

Dr. M told me that the claims were totally exaggerated. In his mind, until recently, the affair had been between two consenting adults and entirely voluntary. The patient was on minimal medications and had originally initiated the sex. Now, however, the doctor was acutely aware that such defenses were weak under the circumstances; he realized the seriousness of the situation and needed legal help.

This was new territory for me. I had sued doctors for malpractice, not defended them! Little did I know that this case would be of critical importance to me. It marked the beginning of my education and inquiry into the powerful forces of transference and projection, as well as the possible adaptation of these forces into the courtroom as tools of persuasion. Showing the jury the impact of these forces, and the effect they had on Dr. M, was the only way I could effectively defend him.

Dr. M told me that he had "lost sight" of his responsibility to use transference wisely, manage the patient's transference with him, and resist his own countertransference with her.[11] He admitted that at one time he had thought of the patient and himself to be "in love," but now realized that the relationship had been caused by a distortion of transference and countertransference. He himself was now in therapy with a colleague who had opened him up to understanding this distortion.

Over the next several weeks, Dr. M and I repeatedly went over how a therapist and a patient could become strongly attached. I needed to understand therapy from the therapist's perspective.

He patiently explained to me how transference worked and how the therapist uses transference to help the patient mine repressed thoughts. We discussed how a therapist, in encouraging transference, can sometimes get confused and lose control of the countertransference one naturally feels unconsciously in many cases. In this case, the patient had been so warm, understanding, and giving that Dr. M felt her love as the love of his deceased mother, a special love that he missed.

The doctor told me that he now understood that he had unconsciously projected his mother's love and care onto this patient. Instead of recognizing this as countertransference, he had been so needy that he lost touch with the doctor/patient relationship and his responsibilities.

In order to properly defend him, I had to research the therapeutic relationship between a psychiatrist and a patient. My study of how transference and the unconscious nature of this phenomenon could create a "boundary violation" allowed me to argue that Dr. M's conduct was not intentional but negligent, as he had failed to live up to the standards of a doctor in recognizing the distortion of the transference phenomenon, which caused the unethical conduct.[12]

My reflective theory is that the twin phenomena of *transference* and *projection* naturally occur between the lawyer and the jury. When used within proper boundaries, this may allow the jurors to internally over-

11 In psychology, therapists use transference to encourage a patient to gain insight. Countertransference simply denotes that feelings the therapist has for the patient are also imbued with the therapist's prior significant relationships with parents and others. Therapists are trained to channel these powerful forces appropriately.

12 A "boundary violation" describes a broad swath of potentially unethical conduct. My understanding of how such conduct can be unconscious and, therefore, unintentional was important in dealing with Dr. M's insurance carrier and persuading the company to pay his defense and cover any liability.

come their resistance to the case. So, the lawyer must recognize this deep, unconscious communication and manage the transference, just as a doctor would manage transference in a therapy setting. We can manage transference by our warm and positive attitude, as well as by sticking to the point, being succinct, and always being transparent and genuine.

But what of the *countertransference* problem? Just as Dr. M failed to recognize the feelings he was having for the patient, trial lawyers also must be aware of and not allow distortion to color the way they are communicating. We can't afford to confront jurors who "get under our skin" in voir dire. Recognizing countertransference can keep us from taking the bait, so that we can continue to communicate with positivity, not hostility.

Practicing psychologists and psychiatrists have incredible knowledge and insight about verbal and nonverbal cues. Day after day, they sit down and help patients heal from emotional pain, cope with family and marital problems, and be more effective in all aspects of their lives, often by using transference and projection as tools.

As trial lawyers, we should do the same thing in the courtroom by helping jurors feel comfortable with the tort system—with finding liability and awarding damages not as a punitive measure, but to help our clients live better for the rest of their lives.

Beyond transference there are empathy, therapeutic alliance, and dynamics of group relationships. With awareness of these psychodynamic tools, we can work harder to adapt them to our relationship with the jury. Using the methods therapists deploy to help patients "open up," we can similarly help persuade our jurors to unconsciously experience, in an empathetic manner, the compelling story of the damage and harm our clients have suffered.

In psychology, the key question a therapist is trained to ask is, "What kind of therapy should I render and what kind of therapist should I be for this type of patient to achieve the desired effect?" We should ask ourselves the same question before entering the courtroom. To accomplish the task of awakening ourselves to be better lawyers during trial, even before the trial begins, we should self-analyze what kind of lawyer we need to be and what we need to do *in this trial* to win over the jurors. This necessarily involves a lot of thought about humanity and how we should conduct ourselves in front of the jury.

Dr. M's case never went to trial. The issue became not whether there was liability, but who had to pay the patient. We went to a three-party mediation, which Dr. M and I attended because his insurance company insisted that it had no liability under the intentional act exclusion. Although the insurance lawyer ridiculed my defense that Dr. M was covered because distorted countertransference was a negligent, not intentional, act, in the end the insurance company paid a reasonable amount to the patient.

Chapter 6

Resistance, Repression, and the Jungian Collective Unconscious

A lawyer should always face up to the fact that jurors will begin the trial as patients begin therapy, with natural, unconscious resistance to change the status quo by transferring money from one person to another.

Therapists are trained to understand that a key barrier to reaching patients is *resistance.* This is the tendency of a patient to resist the efforts of the therapist to get beneath the surface. Resistance to therapy is very common, and therapists are trained to gradually strip away the layers of resistance with the methods we will be discussing throughout this book.

Resistance is related to *repression,* another Freudian term, which describes how the conscious mind protects itself from unpleasant or overpowering thoughts of deep relationships and occurrences from the past.

Freud was educated in medicine as a neurologist. He became proficient at hypnosis to treat patients who had unusual neurological symptoms. He noticed that some patients could not be hypnotized, so he asked them to talk to him about their dreams and fantasies. Freud believed there was a hidden mind that people used as a defense mechanism to protect themselves from disturbing memories and thoughts. Dreams and fantasies, in his view, were a reflection of the repressed unconscious mind.

Freud defined the unconscious simply as "the mind outside of the conscious mind."[13] He believed that people repress powerful childhood memories, but that these memories continue to exist in the unconscious and have a powerful effect on the conscious. Repression serves an important role in the development of a person, keeping such traumatic events as separation from the parent below the surface.

13 S. Freud, "The Unconscious," 1915.

The idea of repression is a foundational tenet of Freudian psychiatry. Several treatment modalities arose over the years from this concept and its many permutations. The basic goal is to reveal to the patient how his unconscious leads him to feel or act in certain ways, as well as to uncover any motivations that may not be obvious consciously. In this way, therapists are able to "treat" the patient by allowing him to obtain insight and self-awareness.

As noted above, however, there is resistance to treatment that must be overcome in the process. Therapists must gain the trust of the patient over the weeks, months, or even years of treatment.

Trial lawyers have been largely deficient in overcoming resistance of jurors. This is a difficult task to achieve because we usually do not have weeks or months at our disposal. Nevertheless, recognizing that jurors are repressing difficult memories that may affect current thinking can help us figure out how to gain trust.

Freud developed theories of how a doctor could get underneath the repressed thoughts. He believed that by mining the unconscious, analyzing dreams, and identifying hidden thoughts through free association a patient could gain relevant insight to facilitate healing. The doctor's role, in his view, was to guide the patient through the unconscious.

This process of assisting the patient with gaining insight is the cornerstone of therapeutic alliance, which creates a powerful unified force for the betterment. This alliance between therapist and patient is effectively the same type of alliance that we want to create with jurors. But, we have to overcome resistance quickly, and we don't have the luxury of talking to the jurors about their dreams, fantasies, and unfulfilled desires.

Plaintiff lawyers need to convince jurors of the significance of certain matters that are a mix of facts and emotions. Our opponents instruct them otherwise. Thus, jurors are inevitably asked to choose. They do so both consciously and unconsciously. For too long, lawyers have emphasized and preached conscious critical thinking to jurors without understanding and taking into account the impact of the unconscious on decision-making.

One helpful concept for trial lawyers is the foundational idea of Carl Gustav Jung, a Swiss physician who was Freud's student and colleague. He theorized in the early 1900s that there was a "collective unconscious."

At the time, Freud and others objected to his work, and a schism was created in the pantheon of psychology. Nevertheless, Jung's ideas have survived, and they have particular relevance to our work with juries, as we try to get eight or twelve people of varied age, gender, and background see what we see and feel what we feel, not only individually, but also as a group.

To reach this group at a collective core, we need to convey the unifying truths that all can share, so that the decision is shared by everyone in the group. Only if we can reach the collective core of a jury's most cherished and strongly held beliefs, like compassion and love, can we show how our case furthers this collective unconscious need.

Jung believed in an *evolutionary* unconscious shared by humanity—inherited and identical in all individuals—which describes how the structure of the psyche "organizes experience."[14] In Jung's opinion, the collective unconscious is a product of evolution in the same way that biological traits are evolutionary according to Darwin's theory. So, a job we can perform as lawyers is to show how these core beliefs have evolved over time, paving the way to a verdict that is truly shared and right from the jury's point of view.

By getting to the place where we all share, we can overcome resistance and break down repression, collectively. For example, we are all born of a father and a mother. While familial relationships vary, we can touch every person on a jury if we can show that what has been lost is the safety and security, if not happiness, of the family. Then we can ask for compensation for that loss without appearing greedy or grubby.

To bring this concept to the courtroom, perhaps in voir dire we should always ask jurors about their childhoods and upbringing, as we know how profoundly each may be affected by these shared and deeply evolutionary concepts of repression, transference, unity, and family. The shared experience of religion may be another way we can reach jurors. Many successful trial lawyers quote scripture or talk about biblical events. If you are comfortable doing this, it could be an important solution to resistance and repression.

---

14 C.G. Jung. "The Structure and Dynamics of the Psyche" (Vol. 8) and "The Archetypes and the Collective Unconscious" (Vol. 9), "The Collected Works of C.G. Jung," Princeton University Press, 1968.

Jung also proposed that human personalities can be categorized into the *extrovert* and *introvert* archetypes (as well as other sub-categorizations). Recognizing which jurors belong to which archetype can help us consider how to successfully reach them, especially in voir dire. Extroverts will probably be more likely to lead, so we must be careful about keeping them on the jury. Introverts may be more difficult to bring out in voir dire, so we have to find ways to learn what they think about money and tort reform. If they are against us fundamentally from the start, it may be very difficult to change their outlook without creating an unconscious intuition on their part that we are in the right.

Jung was criticized for his belief in the shared unconscious. Other scientists of the era felt that his theories of the mind were overly mystical. For our struggle to connect to the jury in the courtroom, however, Jung's thoughts are worth considering. Our focus must be on understanding how to organize the mass of information for the jury so they feel it deeply and come to a shared, and desired, conclusion. We need unanimity or a super majority to win our verdicts.

The unconscious is the engine of information processing and most importantly for the trial lawyer, the source of hidden beliefs and fears, which lead to resistance.

Subliminal stimuli are received by the unconscious. If we can reveal and allow these unconscious elements to flourish in a positive manner, guiding the jurors to see how these elements intersect, we can then ask the jury as a group to ally with us and our view of what decision should be made.

Certainly, numerous factors contribute to a trial lawyer's success, such as experience, intelligence, verbal facility, personality, and so on. The list is endless. Nevertheless, learning how to recognize and manage the unconscious of jurors is intrinsic to our responsibility to give our clients the very best and most competent representation possible.

A therapist overcomes resistance to therapy by acknowledging and working empathetically with the resistance to better allow the patient's unconscious to overcome it. Even though a lawyer can no longer talk with jurors after voir dire, he continues to communicate with the jury by the way he acts and the questions he asks witnesses. These must be well thought-out not only as to the facts elicited, but also with regard to the unconscious messages the jurors will receive.

Chapter 7

The Lawyer as Therapist

We lawyers are not immune to the power of the unconscious. We get glimpses of the unconscious in our fantasies and dreams. There are unexplainable epiphanies, intuitive thinking, déjà vu, and moments of clarity about seemingly unfamiliar matters that we all experience. We also have needs that are difficult to set aside. Countertransference with the judge, a juror, or the opposing counsel can be a barrier to our success. Furthermore, we experience our own resistance and repression.

Even dogs have been shown to have an unconscious in the familiar Pavlovian experiments with subliminal stimuli.[15] It is important for trial lawyers to understand that they have an unconscious mind that is working either in tandem or at cross purposes with the critical thinking and communication they are trying to impart to the jury.

Just as our conscious mind is concentrating, learning, sifting, comparing, and deciding, our unconscious is molding it all into something that resonates, accepting or rejecting. The conscious and unconscious are working separately and together, and the more we can influence the two processes to work in harmony and have others receive our information the way we want it received, the better we will do.

In my 30-plus years in front of juries—sitting next to my clients and talking to and listening to judges, lawyers, and witnesses—I have learned that in the courtroom I am both powerful and powerless, a leader and a follower, in control and under others' control. My powerful unconscious feelings can either aid or obstruct me in my work. Communication comes out from the inside. Thus, recognizing and directing those inner feelings positively are central to ultimate success.

15 Although I recognize that some cynics might compare trial lawyers to dogs, this is not my point.

A successful trial lawyer must have great listening skills. Only by listening to others can we understand what our cases are really about. Due to the unconscious overlay that our brains are constantly seeking to place on what we hear, however, listening with full attention can be hard. This, in effect, is the struggle to *concentrate*. How can we *concentrate* better so that we are not distracted by our own unconscious?

When I enter a courtroom for the first time in a jury trial, I have a bundle of positive and negative thoughts, fears, hopes, anxiety, and a competitive surge of energy. I try to organize both my physical and psychic surroundings so that I can address the jury with confidence and grace. I prepare myself for the battle ahead by mentally cataloguing such things as the layout of the courtroom, the names of the courtroom clerks and court reporter, and the personalities and prerequisites of the judge and opposing attorneys.

I make sure that all electronic media is in place and functioning. I make small talk with my client and remind her of the things we have spoken about: the importance of first impressions, that she should not stare at the jurors, that I will be lightly touching her at times throughout the proceedings and she should react positively to that, and that we must act impeccably 24/7 until the verdict is reached and read aloud in the courtroom.

I also feverishly review juror questionnaires and consult with my assistants and trial consultant, if one is there. Through all of this activity and processing, my mind is churning, applying both logic and emotion. How can I recognize and identify what my unconscious mind is doing to me and my performance?

Just before the trial starts, I keep foremost in my mind that shortly a group of potential jurors will enter the courtroom. That group will include the eight or twelve strangers who will ultimately decide the case, my client's future, and my future as well. Therefore, I have to think of them as the most important people in the courtroom. It is the jurors who are primary in the trial—they make the ultimate decision.

As the jurors enter the room, I try to visualize what they are seeing and how they are processing what they see and hear. I know from my study of the unconscious that they are experiencing what they see and hear in various ways, and that what I do can affect their thinking. So, I sit close to my client, look over at her, and smile. I make sure she knows that she should smile back. I try to appear relaxed and confident, friendly and open, and positive.

I do not shuffle papers, look down at the desk, or appear bored or disinterested. I look at the jury as a group and quickly glance at the individual jurors, without staring at any one of them.

The only chance I have to listen to jurors speak is in voir dire; after that, they are silent participants in the trial, watching, listening, experiencing, and learning. Thus, I have to control my own unconscious so I can speak with the jurors effectively, sifting out and separating how I hear what they are saying. Transference has already begun at this point, as jurors are, each in their own way, listening to me with one ear but hearing me with another, unseen ear. Therefore, I try to make a good impression, conversing easily and comfortably. I learned from juror Gail that jurors feel trapped, so I try my best make them feel more comfortable.

I have read trial skills books and attended many seminars on all aspects of trials. I have tried dozens of cases successfully over the years. I have lost some as well. But, each trial begins my career anew. Past accomplishments are meaningless. The only thing that matters in a given moment is how I approach *this* jury and what I can do to win *this* case.

To win a trial, we have to know not only the facts and the law of the case, but also collateral sciences such as sociology, biology, and medicine. We need to have a working knowledge of drama and storytelling, and we need to know something about digital presentation of documents.

The most important thing to know, after these basic trial skills, is psychology and psychiatry—how therapists approach, reach, and treat their patients, as well as how group dynamics and thinking are structured. We need to understand how we are unconsciously experiencing the trial and consider how it appears to the jury, as that will surely affect *their* unconscious.

Jurors are watching us. To this day, I believe I lost a trial because I wasn't well on the last day of the proceedings; I had to go to the bathroom so badly that I ran out of the courtroom in the middle of my opponent's final argument. A juror told me afterward that in deliberations several jurors had wondered what the other lawyer had said that got me so upset that I couldn't bear to hear it. What did my obvious discomfort and erratic behavior signal to the unconscious minds of the jurors? Could a two-week trial be lost because of such an incident? I know now that I should have figured out a way to tell the jury that I needed a bathroom break. We must somehow convey to the jurors everything that we are doing.

One of my opponents, a great trial lawyer for the defense, always tells the jury in voir dire that he is on medication that makes him somewhat shaky. He tells them that if they see his legs shaking, it is the effect of the medication. He doesn't allow the jurors to speculate that his nervousness is reflective of a bad reaction to evidence. This not only tells the jury concrete information about him, but makes the jurors more comfortable with what they are seeing and receiving.

We have to see the trial through the eyes and the minds of the jurors. We have to listen to them in voir dire. This allows us to have a base understanding of what the actual jurors may be thinking and processing.

We must also be aware of the other lawyers, the judge, and the witnesses, along with the effect they have on us. We surely experience transference and countertransference with each of them, as well as with the jurors, so it is important to recognize how this is manifesting in the courtroom and how the jurors are experiencing these relationships.

Nevertheless, let's always remember that it is the jurors, individually and collectively, who are the most important participants in the trial—not the judge, not the parties, and most certainly not the lawyers. We must reach them, ally with them, teach them, and persuade them. All of this begins when they enter the courtroom and see us.

Chapter 8

Using Unity and Psychodynamic Family to Bond with the Jury

The idea that a trial lawyer has only one job, to get money for his client, is way too simplistic. We have to approach the issue of compensation with subtlety and psychodynamically as a part of the picture, not the whole picture. Therefore, our job is more complex—it is to persuade a group of people to *move* money from one side of the table to the other.

While certainly much of this is done unconsciously and intuitively by the more experienced lawyer, knowing how to communicate this ultimate goal with subtlety can help any trial lawyer be effective and persuasive.

The first job of the trial lawyer in the courtroom is to create an alliance with the jury in the same way that a therapist creates an alliance with a patient or a group. Positivity and the effective use of transference can bond the lawyer to the jury in powerful ways. This creates *trust*, which is a primary tool in overcoming resistance.

Of course, a full therapeutic use of transference and a complete therapeutic alliance often take months or years to accomplish, so there is no way any lawyer can achieve a complete therapeutic alliance with a jury in exactly the same way. But, there are some tools we can borrow from therapists to create an alliance—a feeling of family and safety—in the courtroom.

A therapist uses free association, discussion of fantasies and dreams, and humanistic methods of empathy and positive reinforcement to encourage transference and a positive alliance.

In this context, he discusses with the patient early attachments and relationships to reveal the similarities in the emotional feelings the patient is currently experiencing. The therapist thus tries to unify the past and the present in order to allow the patient to gain insight.

While we can't connect to the jurors directly after voir dire, our ability to show a deep *unity* with the client, so that the jury can experience an indirect transference, is the first fundamental building block for creating a positive alliance. Unity equals family, and family is a singularly powerful force that motivates the unconscious.

We should always approach our client and discuss our client in an open and empathetic manner. We can also question our client and our witnesses in a warm, and even loving, manner. These types of acts can lead to an alliance through indirect transference.

Juror interviews have shown that lawyers have a stature and position in the courtroom similar that of a parent or teacher. We need to think about what our fathers did that was good and strong, what our mothers did that was nurturing and warm, and how our teachers in loco parentis made us feel secure and safe, and try to embed these unspoken elements into our presentation of how we view the client.

Let's look at a major white-collar crime case I tried in federal court with six other lawyers as a case in point. This was a federal conspiracy prosecution involving five individuals and 110 counts of fraud by a "male enhancement" company in the direct marketing industry. My client was the IT director of the company. Seven other executives had pleaded guilty to conspiracy and were government witnesses. Four other executives, along with my client, had to defend themselves over a two-month jury trial. The true issue in the trial was whether the business practices of the defendants were so deceptive and exaggerated as to be criminal.

The other lawyers were brilliant at all aspects of the trial, but all of the other defendants were convicted, while my client was acquitted. Even today, I am constantly asked how this could have happened. What did I do differently? Was it just a weak case against my client compared to the others? Or, was I able to create a three-part trial alliance with my client and the jury in a way that the other lawyers didn't?

The judge clearly thought that I had achieved this. He was an 87-year-old district judge, a very distinguished 30-year veteran of the federal bench. He and I had dinner at a bar association event several weeks after the verdict. I asked him why he thought my client had been acquitted. As this was a very controversial and public case, other lawyers at the table joined in. Everyone wanted to know why my client "got off," when the others were found guilty?

The judge got a sparkle in his eye and said, "Bruce flirted with the jury." Now, clearly I did not "flirt" in the colloquial sense. So, what the judge felt has to be placed into context of the unconscious, psychodynamic level. My construction of what the judge meant by "flirting" was that I had successfully created a transferential trial alliance with the jury as part of our "family," creating a bond that included the jury and my client.

From the very beginning of the trial, in voir dire and my opening, I was brief but informative and showed great care for my client, a young man from India. I spoke about my client's parents, telling the jury that his father was a teacher and his mother stayed at home to look after the kids. I told them about the caste system in India, that my client was a member of the warrior caste whose historical job was to guard the temple and priests, and that his caste was highly valued for honesty, as well as ferocity. This created a sense of family.

But that was not enough. The other defendants presented family matters as well.

The difference, I think, was the projected feeling of *unity*. Throughout the trial, I showed unity with my client—in the courtroom, in the hallway, and even outside the courthouse. He and I were always together. My client was quite a bit younger than me, and the projection I sought to convey was that of father and son. I made sure his fealty to his parents and his ancestry was positively described, and I invited the jury to unconsciously accept him into our collective American family.

Although we were on trial with other co-defendants, I instructed my client not to converse with the other lawyers or defendants in the presence of the jury. While I could control his and my own behavior and transference, I had no control over the others. I wanted to create an image in the jury's mind of unity and family between my client and me. We always conducted ourselves impeccably and did not involve ourselves in any of the petty posturing and arguing that some of the other lawyers engaged in with the judge and the federal prosecutors.

My client did not testify. The jury, therefore, had to gain an intuitive feeling about his character and motivation. So, what the judge called "flirting" had simply been my attempt at using both trial skills and basic positive transference and projection to create a trial alliance sufficiently powerful to allow the jury to feel intuitively comfortable with letting my client walk out a free man.

Once we have transferred to the jury a strong sense of family and unity, we can begin to rely on the jury to develop intuition about the case, unconsciously. If we can do that, success will surely follow.

Chapter 9

Intuition and Hinting as Psychodynamic Tools

Intuition is a mysterious thing. Very little is known about how intuition works, but many have studied it. Intuition is often defined as "understanding without apparent effort" and "keen and quick insight." The word itself is derived from a Latin verb meaning "to contemplate, to look inside."

Intuition is widely felt to be the product of the unconscious mind. There has been a recent spike in interest on this topic among academic psychologists, business psychologists like Gary Klein, the author of "Intuition at Work,"[16] and "New Age" practitioners. While the work in this area is still evolving, scholars have been interested in intuition for a long, long time.

In his work in the 1920s, Jung defines intuition as "perception via the unconscious."[17] He describes the phenomenon as "understanding without conscious recourse to thought, observation, or reason."[18] Intuition became part of Jung's four functions of personality.

Later, at Yale University in the 1970s, Giannini and others also published important articles on the topic, such as "Intellect vs. Intuition: A Dichotomy in the Reception of Nonverbal Communication."[19]

Intuition is currently used as a personality indicator, or "axis," in the commonly used Myers-Briggs personality test. It has also been described as a function of the right brain and abstract thinking. This follows the

16 G. Klein. "Intuition at Work: Why Developing Your Gut Instincts Will Make You Better at What You Do," Doubleday Business, 2002.

17 C. G. Jung. "Psychological Types," Rutledge and Keegan Paul, London, 1923.

18 Id.

19 A. J. Giannini, J. Daood, M. C. Giannini, R. Boniface, and P. G. Rhodes. Journal of General Psychology, 99, 19–24, 1978.

Jungian theory that certain personalities function from intuition, rather than thinking, feeling, or sensation.

Intuition has been associated with divine inspiration, as well as scientific discovery. In recent years, spiritualist Deepak Chopra wrote a book called "The Power of Intuition," which describes intuition as a mystery that leads to greater understanding by looking for answers inside, rather than seeking external evidence.

According to Webster's Dictionary, the synonyms for intuition are discernment, perception, instinct, and inspiration.

Intuition is a very powerful phenomenon in the courtroom, as it invites jurors to find the answers from within. While presenting an organized and honest argument based on evidence is the central skill of a trial lawyer, the transfer of intuitive thinking to the jury is the next step toward excellence, since people believe most fervently the things they have internalized.

Intuition is the most direct route to reach the jurors' unconscious, leading them to come to a conclusion from the inside, rather than by the more obvious but less powerful conscious review of the evidence.

Before we can influence a jury's intuition, however, we have to accurately assess and evaluate our own unconscious and our own intuition about the case. This is difficult to do and typically requires a firm knowledge of the science and psychology of jury trials, as well as input from others, such as focus groups. Only then, with this backdrop of thought, study, and preparation, can we effectively use intuition to persuade.

So, how can we encourage a jury to engage in intuitive thinking that favors our point of view? The single most important psychodynamic tool for a trial lawyer is what I call *hinting*, which Webster's defines as a "brief and indirect statement of what is to come."

Some years ago, I had a trial in which the defendant, a driver, was alleged to have been talking on a cell phone at the time she had struck my client, a pedestrian. My hinting in this context was to tell the jury early in the trial: "Ladies and gentlemen, you will find later in this trial that a cell phone will take on importance in this case. Please be on the lookout for evidence about a cell phone."

This hinting did several things. First, my asking the jury to remember something touched the unconscious collective in a fundamental manner. Second, the jury could easily identify with a cell phone, an item that is ubiquitous in today's world. Third, because I didn't directly explain the importance at the time, but promised to later, I was able to prompt the jury's intuitive thinking to begin to organize the information along with other facts.

Lawyers must train themselves to use hinting to encourage jurors' intuition about the ultimate issues of the case. If we get to the end of the trial and the jury's intuition is in our favor, we have won.

Along with presenting the values of family and unity, hinting is a fundamental way to spark and influence a jury's intuition.

Chapter 10

The Humanistic Lawyer and Courtroom as a Community

In order to open jurors to accept and internalize our hints, as well as our showing of family values and unity, we must prepare them to be open to unconscious transference from the beginning of the trial. Once again, scholars in psychology and trial consulting provide a valuable and underused resource for the psychodynamic trial lawyer.

An important modern offshoot of Freudian and Jungian theories is the humanistic concept of psychologist Carl Rogers. His theories of psychotherapy can be very useful to the trial lawyer in how to approach the jury and the unconscious of the jury. Rogers is the father of the "counseling" model of psychotherapy, which is less time-consuming and more oriented to specific problem-solving than psychoanalysis.

Rogers wrote that all individuals perceive themselves at the center of experience. What we should learn from this is that each juror, though part of a group, is experiencing the trial as an individual and reacting to the trial as it relates to him. The challenge, then, is to either merge the individual with the group, in order to allow a humanistic sense of community to forge the way to remedy, or to make the individual feel that the remedy must be one that will help not only the injured party, but also the juror, his or her family, and community at large.

These alternate concepts happen to intersect with ideas in the recent book by Peter Block on the individual contribution to corporate community building[20] and trial skill theories propounded by trial consultant David Ball and his co-author and collaborator, trial lawyer Don Keenan.[21]

20 P. Block. "Community: The Structure of Belonging," Barrett-Koehler Publishers Inc., 2008.

21 D. Ball and D. Keenan. "Reptile," Balloon Press, 2009.

According to Block, individuals must feel that they belong and are part of the fabric of the greater corporate community in order to be effective. The same holds true for jurors: each individual must feel empowered to express his or her feelings in order for the group to act humanely and humanistically. The trial lawyer must make the courtroom a community, with the jury at the center.

We can tap the psychodynamic unconscious of the jury in these positive ways by using early therapeutic methods developed by Rogers in his work on what he calls "client-based counseling."[22]

Rogers states that there are three core conditions that allow a therapist to succeed in helping a client (i.e., patient) with everyday issues and problems:

1. The therapist must approach the client with unconditional positive regard.
2. There must be congruence between the therapist and the client, which is achieved by authenticity, genuineness, and transparency.
3. The therapist must approach the client with empathetic understanding.

It is easy to see how these principles, used to achieve a therapist's goal, are similar to what we, as trial lawyers, should attempt to achieve in the courtroom. We should approach the trial itself, voir dire of the jurors, and direct examination of the witnesses for our side with the three core conditions urged by Rogers.

If we approach the trial in a humanistic manner, with authenticity, genuineness, and transparency, hold the jury in unconditional positive regard, and display genuine empathetic understanding of the harm suffered by our client, how can the jurors turn us down when we ask them to do the unusual and give our client "B" money from the defendant "A"?

It would be a lot easier to do this if there was simply a pot of money belonging to the court, or a totally neutral entity, that the jury could simply give to our client. The truth is, however, that we are asking for a transfer of wealth. This is not only counterintuitive, but also a political football in today's culture war between the conservative and liberal camps.

---

22 C. Rogers. "Client-Centered Therapy: Its Current Practice, Implications, and Theory," Houghton-Mifflin, Boston, 1951.

Because this is not merely an abstraction but a very real concern, we need to allow jurors to intuitively reach a state of mind that enables them to do this in a humanistic manner. Jurors often feel trapped and under tremendous pressure. By using Rogers' positive methods to show the same compassion toward the jury as we display toward our client, we can allow the jurors to put themselves in our shoes.[23]

By combining the community concept of humanism with positive transference, we can achieve the desired effect—the intuitive sense by the jury as a group that it is important and safe to rule in favor of our client, and that it is okay and proper for them as jurors to give another person's money as compensation. This is an important psychodynamic solution to the "Peter and Paul" dilemma that every juror faces.

23 This positive regard is similar to but not the same as "repetitive positive reinforcement," a concept championed by B.F. Skinner to show that animals (and humans) can be trained to act in desired ways by getting treats, favorite toys, etc.

Chapter 11

Group Dynamics—Arming and Empowering Empathetic Jurors

A therapist deals one-on-one with a patient over a long period of time. A lawyer does not have the same luxury when dealing with a jury. Most of the trial is conducted with the jury listening, assembling, and *deciding* as a group, both in the jury box and in the deliberation room.

This is where a working knowledge of the body of research in group dynamics can be helpful. In addition to facilitating the development of positive intuition about the case, it can enable us to give the jurors on our side the tools necessary to persuade the other jurors.

All trial lawyers know that a jury is the quintessential group of eight or twelve individuals thrown together for a common purpose. The group is formed and chosen by the lawyers from a larger pool. The act of being "chosen" in itself creates a powerful impression on the jurors.

The voir dire is the first part of a trial, but many initial impressions are formed by the unconscious of the jury even before the voir dire. At voir dire, jurors may feel that they are being interviewed for a job. Thus, when they are chosen, *empowerment* begins. This factor is especially important because of the difficult thing we are asking the jurors to do. We want to encourage their feeling of specialness, as this will allow us to ask them to do an extraordinary thing.

When we stand before a jury for our opening statement, we are shooting off signals that are being received by the jurors individually and as a group. A group is more than the sum of its parts. Research has clearly shown that groups act in certain ways. We have to be aware of the dynamic of the group, as well as the individual jurors, if we want to use our communicative and intuitive skills in an effective manner.

Group dynamics is a core concept of psychology, sociology, business, advertising, politics, and criminal justice. Freud wrote a book called "Group Psychology and the Analysis of the Ego." Carl Rogers studied group behavior. Warren Bennis, the guru of leadership, likewise studied and wrote on group dynamics.[24] The list of multidisciplinary researchers in this area is long and distinguished.

Wilfred Bion, M.D., a British psychiatrist and researcher, is considered the father of modern group theory. His book about his work in the post-World War II era with traumatized soldiers at the Tavistock Institute in England, "Experiences in Groups," outlines his idea that in groups the analytic model is not to cure but to search for the truth.[25]

Bion believed that there are two groups within every group: a "work group" that is anchored to the basic task at hand and another unit that, like the unconscious, is influenced by the basic assumptions of the group and acts in dynamic ways. Bion believed that an effective group would meld the Beta (unconscious) with the Alpha (conscious/critical thinking) to rationally solve the basic task.

He postulated that there were three basic assumptions that could manifest in any given group: dependency, anti-dependency, and pairing.

In case of *dependency*, a group relies on the leadership of one individual. It depends on one leader to make decisions and follows the leader.

A corollary of this is *anti-dependency*, which manifests when a group turns against its leader. An example of this type of group dynamic often shown at meetings and seminars is the movie and play, "Twelve Angry Men."

Most trial lawyers would like to avoid either of these groups. The conventional wisdom is to get any strong leader types off the jury because a strong leader can lead the jury against you. If we can identify a leader who will support us for strong unconscious reasons, however, we should always try to keep him on the jury, as he will almost certainly guarantee a favorable verdict.

---

24 W. G. Bennis and H. A. Shepard. "A Theory of Group Development," Journal of Human Relations, 9(4), 415–437, 1956; W. G. Bennis and P. W. Biederman, "Organizing Genius: The Secrets of Creative Collaboration," Addison-Wesley Publishing Company, 1996.

25 W. R. Bion. "Experiences in Groups," Basic Books, 1951.

If you have not been able to challenge an unfriendly leader type, the clear choice is to somehow isolate her and help create an anti-dependency group. One way to do this is by *arming* the jury in the final argument with a direction to go in the event of an attempted takeover by a leader who opposes a favorable verdict.

Arming is the direct appeal to friendly jurors to reject attempts from unfriendly jurors to introduce negative elements into the deliberations. Here, we present the jurors with a basis to discuss positive evidence and facts, while explicitly asking them to take action and verbally reject any sabotage by an unfriendly juror.

Arming starts at voir dire. I always make sure each juror agrees that in the event another juror starts to criticize the plaintiff, our witnesses, or me because of some extraneous reason, he or she will speak up to defend us and get the deliberations back on track to determine proper compensation.

Of course, we cannot always know if there is a strong leader who may dominate the jury and ultimately make the decision. That is one reason we tell jurors to ignore and reject any attempts to hijack deliberations.

Social and professional status is an important factor in determining leadership, so we should act with great caution in deciding whether to leave a highly educated or wealthy juror on a jury. We need to spend more time with these jurors in voir dire to find out how they were brought up, whether they have had family members harmed by other persons, and whether they have a bias about the tort system, along with other factors that may significantly impact juror decision-making.

The third group assumption identified by Bion is *pairing*. In this case, two members of a group pair off and form an alliance with each other. The pair may have great influence over the decision of the group, often ending up doing the work of the group. Of course, we have no way of knowing at voir dire whether there will be such a pair on the jury or who that pair may be. If there are two jurors who are very similar in age, dress, occupation, and other characteristics, however, we should take note and at least prepare ourselves for a possible pairing if we keep them on the jury.

That is why I recommend carefully watching jurors' conduct outside the courthouse to the greatest extent possible. If you identify a pair who spend all of their time together, who go to lunch together every day, and arrive at the courthouse and walk out together most days, you probably have a pairing—and this pair may well decide the case.

In this case, you want to learn everything you can about the pair and try to create positive transference with them through your conduct during the trial. You can do this by the way you treat your client, the questions you ask witnesses, and your nonverbal communication with the jurors. A pair can be powerful in deliberations, so if you have one, you need to address them at final argument, acknowledge that they are a pair, and ask them to speak up for your client as a pair in the deliberations. Combining knowledge about group dynamics and arming can empower you to position a pair of jurors to win over the others and carry the day.

Another thing to consider is how your jury may be dealing with the fight or flight instinct. Bion felt that many groups have a fight or flight personality. A *fight* group is aggressive and hostile, with people fighting with each other. We have all had cases where the clerk or the bailiff would tell us, "The jurors have been yelling at each other all morning." A *flight* group is avoidance-oriented and will engage in small talk or go off topic in order to avoid the basic task at hand.

Such groups probably do not have a strong leader or pair to do the work of the group, so they either avoid the task altogether or become hostile and fight about the work. If you have a fight or flight group that is taking an extraordinarily long time, consider finding a reason to ask the judge to bring the jury back into the courtroom for further instruction.

This is why arming is essential when dealing with jury group dynamics. If you have armed the jury in the final argument with certain critical instructions, your jurors will almost certainly remember and be able to renew their use of the instructions to persuade the others.

PART II

The Scientific Courtroom

Chapter 12

Emerging Science of Jury Trials

I started practicing law in the late 1970s. During those years, the training I received as an eager young trial lawyer was to be well prepared, be careful about what you say in jury selection so as not to pollute the jury, be as charming and winning a personality as you could muster, and bring the case home with a brilliant final argument. I tried dozens of public defender and auto accident cases to skeptical juries.

The science of a jury trial was not on the radar screen. Seminars focused on mechanics of the various aspects of the trial, but very little was taught about the relationships in the courtroom—and nothing at all about the forms of communication between lawyer and jury.

My training was very superficial and basic, and often the exact opposite of the methods we now routinely use. For example, the prevailing theory of voir dire at that time urged trial lawyers to try to propagandize jurors and "sell the case," while concentrating on preventing jurors from get "polluted" by other prospective jurors. These ideas have since been generally discredited.

It is now well accepted that the purpose of voir dire is to identify tort reformers or other "enemies" and try to get them off the jury, and that juror values are so deeply rooted that "polluting" by discussing things like frivolous lawsuits is not a real risk.

While the most famous trial lawyers such as Melvin Belli from San Francisco, Ed Rood from Florida, Philip Corboy from Chicago, Gerry Spence from Wyoming, Scott Baldwin from Texas, and David Shrager from Philadelphia were widely regarded as courtroom magicians, little was known about why they were so successful, other than their drive, intelligence, and outsized personalities. We admired them for their success.

These giants would on occasion present seminars at the ATLA conventions. They would talk about how they charmed juries, with anecdotes about developing and giving opening statements and, most importantly, convincing juries with great eloquence and emotion in final argument to bring home the big verdict. They were giants of the bar, and as young lawyers we tried to emulate their accents and mannerisms, believing that if we could just talk like them and act like them, then we would also be successful.

The best "how-to" books available before quite recently, beyond the technical texts of evidence rules and civil procedure and early manuals like McElhaney's on cross-examination, were essentially war stories, verbatim opening statements, and final arguments that the most successful lawyers had delivered in their million-dollar verdicts. The idea that there was a unifying way to try a case, from voir dire to jury instructions, was not in common parlance.

The first time I saw a science-based trial method discussed that transcended charismatic personal attributes was at a Trial Lawyers Convention seminar given by Rood in the early 1980s. Rood was an older man with a distinct and charming southern twang; his voice was like a burbling stream—warm and seductive.

Rood's thesis was that jurors would negotiate with each other about damages, especially for pain and suffering. Therefore, he recommended that at final argument we ought to *always* prepare a chart with a range of damages for each element of pain and suffering allowable, from a higher number that was considerably more than what we actually wanted to a lower number that we actually wanted. Rood told us that in his long experience, the jury would either come back with a verdict between the two numbers or at the lower number.

Jurors had to see the chart; it was not enough to simply tell them the damages. "Make the chart big," Rood told us, "Put it right in front of the jury box and use a pointer to go down your two alternative lists." This, of course, is what we now call "arming," giving those jurors favorable to our case a number to negotiate from.

Since that time, and particularly over the past 10 years, there has emerged a growing science of jury trials, driven by trial and jury consultants like Amy Singer of Florida, Lisa Blue from Texas, and my cohorts,

Mark Modlin and Becky Jones of Kentucky. More recently, publisher Trial Guides out of Portland has published extremely helpful guides, such as trial books by Ball and Don Keenan on damages, Rick Friedman's and Patrick Malone's "Rules of the Road," and others.

It is now clear that there are known methods that can increase the chances of success with juries. Furthermore, such methods have been proven to work—at least anecdotally. This is what I call "the emerging science of jury trials." However, simply reading books is not enough to know and effectively implement this emerging science. It is imperative to understand the psychological underpinnings of human behavior and communication, in order to begin the process of learning how to tap into the unconscious of the jurors in an effective way.

Why do I call this "science"? Because by using these carefully created methods and understanding how they actually work psychodynamically, different lawyers can obtain similar successful verdicts. The very definition of scientific methodology is that a hypothesis can be proven at different places and times following the same process and procedure. This is called *reproducibility*.

The Internet and the age of computerization have given us the ability to communicate and discover information rapidly and widely. We now have the ubiquitous list serve, which allows trial lawyers statewide, nationwide, and even worldwide to share information about their trials with all who are interested. From the list serves and other publications, we are told that thousands of dedicated trial lawyers everywhere have read the works or attended the workshops of Ball and Keenan, or have been to the Spence College in Wyoming.

Trial consultants have also begun to help trial lawyers with mock trials and focus groups, in order to mimic the courtroom experience before the trial. By asking focus groups to talk about trial-related issues, they've found that certain attitudes exist prevalently among jurors. For example, participants across the board had a negative reaction to million-dollar verdicts for apparently frivolous claims, like that of the woman burned by hot coffee at McDonald's.

Another key finding suggests that propaganda by the insurance companies and the Chamber of Commerce is effective. Trial consultants have reported that if jurors with negative attitudes are acknowledged but told that the case at hand is not frivolous, these cynical jurors could be open to a verdict for money damage awards.

Furthermore, these efforts have revealed that jurors have a negative attitude toward legal lingo. They often feel that lawyers act superior and confuse them with words and phrases that virtually no one other than lawyers understands.

The trial consultants found that if lawyers used everyday words, such as "before" instead of "prior" and "after" instead of "subsequently," jurors felt more comfortable and open to the lawyers' ideas and contentions. Friedman wrote that jurors were more comfortable deciding about "rules," instead of more obscure things like "standard of care."

Taking these lessons from the emerging trial law science and learning the principles of transference, projection, and intuition to persuade jurors—by allowing them to reach conclusions from within, rather than by a vast recitation of facts and confusing legal doctrines remote from everyday life—can empower trial lawyers to consistently win cases and gain proper compensation for their clients.

Chapter 13

"Scientific" Lawyers and Trial Consultants

Lawyers like Spence and Keenan and consultants like Ball are aiming to prove that there is a scientific basis for such things as asking jurors on voir dire to convey their attitudes about tort reform and damages, and that this would not "pollute" the jury. They advise using "harm" to describe loss, rather than "pain and suffering," using the scales of justice in every case to visually describe the burden of proof, and using vulnerability and transparency in approaching the jury on voir dire. Studying their theories and recommendations can help us learn and incorporate the science of jury trials into our own work.

Spence, the Freudian Lawyer

Gerry Spence, the great trial lawyer from Wyoming, emphasizes the importance of letting the jury know that you, the lawyer, love your client. He also says to tell the jury upfront of your fear of losing. This is to gain empathy for the client through empathy for you.

This is exactly the way transference works in the field of psychology to help patients open up and overcome natural resistance to therapy. By using the methods of therapists—transference, unconditional positive regard, mirroring, and hinting—we can quickly and effectively achieve the empathy we need to win cases.

One case I tried years ago was a successful defense of a young nurse, Tracey, who had been wrongfully accused of stealing drugs from the hospital. The hospital security director had intercepted her, searched her, and although he found nothing, called the police. She was handcuffed and arrested in front of her colleagues, and spent a night in jail before her fiancé bailed her out. The hospital summarily fired her.

After we won her acquittal on all 18 counts at the criminal trial, we sued the hospital and police for malicious prosecution and false arrest. Tracey was completely traumatized by the arrest and termination of her employment. The hospital hired a former prosecutor, "Tom M.," who was now practicing at a leading insurance defense firm, as its defense counsel.

The trial was electric and competitive, led by a veteran judge named "the Crusher" for his punitive sentencing of criminal defendants. The defense attorney spent most of the trial focused on me, ridiculing me for my long hair, my audacity to bring such a frivolous lawsuit to trial, and his characterization of me as a "criminal lawyer." Tom was a handsome and a skilled orator. He obviously felt that he had the trial won as soon as he'd walked into the courtroom.

At that time, I had just finished reading Spence's first book, "Gunning for Justice." Following its guidance, I showed the jury how much I cared for Tracey and her family. I sat close to her in a protective way at our table and always responded to her whispered questions with patience and a smile. By my questions, the jury knew that I viewed Tracey with high and positive regard and that I cared deeply about her. I also let the jury know that I was familiar with Tracey's parents and fiancé, speaking with them frequently during breaks in the jury's presence and eyesight.

After one week of trial, I looked forward to some private time with my wife and two infant sons over the weekend, but I had to attend a fundraiser for another judge—a fancy cocktail party. This was a big trial, and in the courthouse word travels fast. A lot of the lawyers and some of the judges were very interested in how the trial was going. Several of them mentioned that Tom, my adversary, had regaled them earlier with his perception of the trial: "Whitman is in love with his client. He is obsessed with her, blind to the truth. There is no way he is going to get anything in this case."

He was right: I did "love" Tracey. But he was wrong about the rest. My "love" for my client was being unconsciously and intuitively received by the jury in a very positive light, in great contrast with Tom's negativity and caustic lack of regard. The jurors felt the unity between me, my client, and her family. At the same time, they were put off by Tom's rude and arrogant conduct in the courtroom.

When the jury came back after several hours of deliberations, the verdict was loud and clear: *One Million Dollars.* And then, after the clerk had read the verdict forms, the most remarkable thing happened. The jurors came over to our table, some with tears in their eyes, hugged Tracey and me, and thanked me for helping her.

We cannot overlook or underappreciate the great effect Gerry Spence and his vulnerability methods have added to trial science. Although many think of Spence as a flamboyant, charismatic, long-haired cowboy, his books, articles, and seminars, beginning in the early 1980s with "Gunning for Justice," have advised us as lawyers to display not only our strength, but also vulnerability and humanity to the jury.

Spence was the early pioneer in projection, transference, and awakening the repressed unconscious, the trial lawyer who acted as a Freudian therapist, helping the jury feel empathy by providing empathic and positive reinforcement from the beginning of the trial.

In his approach, Spence is the embodiment of the Freudian theory of the unconscious. He is asking the jurors to examine and expel their repressed fears and traumas by revealing his own. He overcomes their resistance by showing his fears and weaknesses, as though he is a child and the jury is his collective, Jungian parent. Spence allows the jury to see him as powerful and vulnerable at the same time, as the father and the child. He begs for help, and he pleads for their verdict.

This is classic transference. It is not something that only Spence can do; with compassion, genuineness and intent, any trial lawyer can achieve transference in approaching a jury. It requires acceptance of the therapeutic model. A lawyer who cannot overcome the need for control and self-aggrandizement (which most of us have) will not be able to use this methodology.

Ball and Rogerian Empathy

Trial consultant David Ball, in his very important book for trial lawyers, "Damages," teaches that there is a need to view the trial as Rogers viewed the therapeutic experience—as a process experienced by a group of individuals, with each juror seeing himself or herself at the center of the experience. Ball is convinced that the lawyer's presentation and demeanor are important for how the individual juror views the trial.

Ball suggests that we dress in modest suits and cheap shirts and ties. We should not be flamboyant at all and let the jury be the center of the focus, in a sense using the model of behavioral therapy, rather than analysis. In this, Ball differs from the more Freudian approach of Spence, who is flamboyant in his dress and speaking manner and who seeks to be the center of the experience and project a strong father figure, as well as a subservient and childlike persona.

Ball is more maternal in his unconscious approach to the jury. He suggests that we use our hands in shaping and emphasizing verbal points to bring jurors into our sphere in a more subtle way. He encourages lawyers to step away from the podium and stand in front of the jury, as close as is allowed and comfortable, without any physical barriers between them and the jury.

Ball says when we are speaking to the jury or a central witness, we should open our arms widely. The psychodynamic meaning of this is that it evokes transference, opens us up, and makes us appear transparent. This is maternal and nurturing. It is also vulnerable in a nonverbal way.

The most powerful presentation, in my view, should unify trial science and psychology. We can do so by following some of the emerging principles, such as those described in the "Rules of the Road," using voir dire to remove tort reformers, and, at the same time, learning and implementing psychodynamic methods such as transference and projection to enhance empathy and intuition.

Chapter 14

Convergence of Jury Science and Psychodynamics

How can we use emerging science taught by Spence, Ball, and others while applying psychodynamic effects to create positive unconscious cognition among jurors?

One thing I always do is arrive at the courthouse with my client before the jury arrives. I make sure my client is within eyesight of the door through which jurors enter the courthouse every day, especially during deliberations, to show the jury that we are there as early as they are, that we care, and that we have not moved on to other matters. We do this even in freezing weather, standing outside until jurors have seen us.

This is a non-negotiable point. Like parents, my client and I are there when jurors leave at night and when they arrive in the morning. This creates unconscious cues that can lead to a powerfully favorable transference and intuition for our side.

However, we have to use therapeutic methods with great care. Some lawyer behaviors can harm the transferential experience and lead to a negative transference, prompting a juror to unconsciously view the lawyer not as a loving and caring parent, but as the parent who doesn't care or whom the juror feared or hated. This is the transference we don't want to occur. Examples of bad conduct by lawyers are endless, but there are some obvious things we need to watch out for and refrain from doing while any juror may be present.

First, don't ever yell at your client or someone in his family. Don't flippantly ignore your client at counsel table when she asks you something. Don't immediately jump on your cell phone in the hallway during breaks in a place where jurors might see you. Don't rush away or obviously move to another case in front of any jurors. Don't ignore a juror where you see him, no matter what the judge has instructed. These behaviors destroy the sense of unity and family we are trying to achieve.

In transference, we want to be the good parent, the loving grandfather, the helpful older sister, or the vulnerable child, not the diffident parent, the remote or angry grandfather, or the bullying older brother. Our goal is to let the jury come to an unconscious and intuitive decision, a "gut feeling" that we are the good and the right side. That is how we win jury trials—not just by the rote invocation of the "rules of the road" or "reptilian" themes.

In a sense, we are in a play, acting as providers of information, psychologists, event planners, and entertainers. We have to control the external environment as well as we can, so that our courtroom presentation is genuine on the inside. Always remember and tell all participants on your side that the trial expands outside the courtroom. The jurors are watching everything, not just what we put on screens or whom we bring onto the witness stand. The unconscious of the jury does not turn off when they leave the courtroom.

Of course, we cannot totally control the trial or the courtroom itself. We have to recognize and respect—and show the jury that we respect—the other forces of control. These include, first and foremost, the judge and his staff, as well as the opposing lawyer. Our transference with the judge is seen and evaluated by the jury. The judge's regard for us and the other side has a profound influence on the jurors; they experience a powerful transference with the judge and undoubtedly have a parental regard for him or her.

Our flexibility in dealing with the opposing counsel and the power of the judge is critical to our success in positive unconscious communication with the jury. The courtroom is no place for lawyers who have an emotional need to control everything or engage in constant conflict with the judge. Others have written extensively about how to handle judges who are oppositional, who dog us with rebukes in front of the jury, or who ridicule our evidence or express doubt as to our witnesses' credibility.

Many believe we must confront and slay the bad judge. However, this is extremely difficult. Plus, there may be unconscious repercussions against lawyers who are constantly at odds with the judge.

We can save any criticism of the judge for our final argument, acknowledging that we've had some difficulties, but that the jury need only consider our struggle with the judge as a personal battle we've had to deal with. If we can admit our inadequacy in dealing with the judge, the parent, perhaps we can unconsciously create a stronger alliance with the collective unconscious of the jurors, who have their own struggles with parents, bosses, and spouses. However, this should only come up in the final part of our final argument, so we do not distract ourselves from our focus on the jury and what they are experiencing.

Countertransference can be your enemy. Transference is a two-way street, and like Dr. M we can destroy ourselves with unrecognized countertransference. In therapy, unconscious countertransference might result in the therapist seeking a close personal or even sexual relationship with a patient. In a courtroom, unconscious countertransference can lead to disastrous dealings with the judge or a particular juror, leading to an Oedipal power struggle that can distract the trial lawyer from the job and lose the case.

In the federal conspiracy trial I discussed earlier, one of my co-counsel, a brilliant, Harvard-trained trial lawyer of great reputation and oratorical skill, got stuck and distracted in his unconscious struggle with the judge, also Harvard-trained. As a result, the lawyer lost sight of how his defense was being heard by the jury—how they were experiencing him and his client. He felt he was "winning" the Oedipal struggle with the judge and, therefore, must be winning the trial. This led to the poor decision not to present any defense at all and rely solely on the failure of the burden of proof. I believe that every other lawyer in the trial questioned this, but as the lead attorney my co-counsel had the final say. The jury convicted his client of over 100 counts of fraud and conspiracy.

From the psychodynamic perspective, a therapist would similarly distort the therapeutic alliance if he tried to compete with or intrude into the patient's parental memories. We always need to keep aware of our inner Oedipus, recognize it as what it is, and fight the urge to destroy the judge.

Chapter 15

Effective Use of Trial Consultants

Great marketing companies like Procter & Gamble constantly test products with focus groups, surveys, and other methods. These are more or less scientific ways to find out what a demographic thinks about all aspects of a given product.

Over the past 20 years, trial lawyers like John Edwards and Don Keenan and consultants like David Ball and Mark Modlin have developed ways to get data about all aspects of our trial strategies and theories through the use of pre-trial focus groups. Anecdotally, Edwards would conduct more than 10 focus groups before setting foot in the courtroom for trial.

As it has become more and more difficult to win plaintiff verdicts, we have seen a progressive rise in the use and importance of trial consultants—a relatively new legal discipline that originated with jury experts helping to "select" juries, but has now morphed into a more extensive role with nearly unlimited scope.

Trial consultants help us improve pre-trial preparation and focus group experience by reminding us to keep in mind the psychodynamic aspects of how people think in groups. One of Jung's theories is that we all share an evolutionary *collective unconscious* that acts *exactly alike* in every person. Knowing about and recognizing this idea can be very helpful to us as trial lawyers.

The challenge, of course, is finding where in our case we can tap into this collective unconscious. Trial lawyers Friedman and Malone, in "Rules of the Road," teach that a trial lawyer must determine simple, universal rules of the case and base the entire trial on how the defendant broke the rules.[26] Rules, therefore, become embedded in the collective unconscious.

26 R. Friedman and P. Malone. "Rules of the Road," Trial Guides, 2006.

This theory prompts a number of practical questions. How do we find out what the rules are and apply them to a specific case? Are there universal Jungian rules that we can use in every case? How do jurors learn the rules? Do they process information better by seeing the rule stated or displayed on boards and screens, or by indirectly inferring or intuitively realizing it from the inside?

Another issue is to define the actual question we are asking the jury to consider. Author and corporate consultant Peter Block writes that there are "how" questions that stifle the ability to act in a positive fashion, by inhibiting action, and there are "yes" questions that encourage positive action, community, and overcoming fear.[27] We need to be open to asking jurors to answer "yes" questions that allow actions, not those "how" questions that block empathy, creativity, and remedy.

Trial consultants Mark Modlin and Becky Jones are well known to lawyers in Kentucky, Ohio, Indiana, and Pennsylvania, as well as other parts of the country. They often help me prepare for trial.

Modlin is a former Christian youth minister and psychologist by training. He came to trial consulting after a stint as a jail warden in Newport, Kentucky. He is shrewd and calculating, as well as controversial among lawyers, with some incorrectly believing that his settlement efforts play both sides of a case. Beneath his calculating exterior, however, is a deep concern for the injured, the sick, and the helpless, as well as their lawyers, who are often out of pocket for thousands of dollars and untold hours on exceedingly difficult cases.

Modlin says there is a difference between the "human value" and the "legal value" of the case. The human value is the value of the case to the client. It includes all of the harm and places a high value on such things as pain and suffering and the inability to engage in normal daily activities.

The legal value is the value the law places on the case, assuming liability. It includes an analysis of the percentage of risk of winning the trial, the time-value of money, and the controversy over tort cases and money damages for injury in general. The legal value, therefore, is lower than the human value and is the rough equivalent of the lowest figure that Rood wrote on the board so many years ago. We have to allow the

27 P. Block. "The Answer to How Is Yes," Barrett-Koehler, 2003.

jury latitude to find and award the legal value. This is a rule that can be applied to every case.

Our challenge is to make the jury come to a verdict for the plaintiff for *at least the legal value,* knowing that this will require the jury to overcome resistance to forcing the defendant to pay the plaintiff money (e.g., the Peter bias). Although we think jurors know that there is insurance in most cases, we can't be sure of that and most courts restrict even the mention of the word "insurance."[28] If we can come to a comfortable argument of what the legal value is and what the jury must award, we can use this collective unconscious comfort to overcome juror resistance.

From another perspective, the legal value analysis is a way of describing how the collective unconscious works to compromise and negotiate to come to a decision on damages.

One way to impact this deeper level of the unconscious is by using the Friedman and Malone method of naming the rule for the jury at the beginning of the trial and then continuing to emphasize that the defendant broke this rule throughout the entire trial. Friedman believes that if we "try the rule," we will be successful once the jury agrees with the rule and that it has been broken. Ball also offers very helpful tips on how to present damages in the context of "harm," rather than as "damages," in order to persuade the jury that the proper measure of money is that which most accurately reflects the harm, and no more.

We need to do this carefully, however, because psychodynamically the Jungian evolutionary unconscious that works exactly the same in all of us can impede empathy for our injured client. It is when we overcome this impediment, according to Modlin, that we can begin to persuade the jury that the real value of the case is closer to the human value, not the legal value.

One powerful way to test the collective unconscious is by trying out theories and rules on focus groups.

Modlin often gets to know my client and the family before we do a focus group. This helps him direct the focus group more deeply and fully, so that we can subsequently use what we have learned more effectively at

28 In Ohio, we allow questions in voir dire about any family members who work in insurance. We have a jury instruction that jurors are not to consider insurance. I recommend using both of these opportunities to set in the jury's mind that there is insurance.

trial. He also interviews my client and the family, sometimes on videotape, to help me understand the harm from a human value point of view. His questions are usually different from mine as a lawyer.

Modlin and Jones work on analogies and one-liners derived from our focus groups for use in the opening statement and final argument. Sometimes they actually write a suggested draft of an opening or final argument. I don't use their suggestions verbatim, but it is surprising how often their recommendations find their way into the trial in one way or another. The idea is that the more the jurors figure out through subtlety and cues like rhetorical questions, rather than me dictating law to them, the more they will be able to use their individual and collective unconscious to persuade themselves through intuitive thinking.

What Modlin has taught me about rules is that a focus group can define a rule for me, rather than vice versa, and he and Jones can then refine it to a one-liner. "If a doctor gives a patient a diagnostic test, and it is abnormal, he must take some action to inform the patient, refer the patient to a specialist, or further test to rule out a dangerous disease." This rule restated to the jury in the opening statement frames the trial and lets the jury go deep into the collective unconscious to figure the harm done by the breaking of the rule.

According to Jones, "Defense lawyers always try the same case, but plaintiff lawyers are always recreating the wheel." The jury knows upfront that the defendant doctor or company will be denying fault; people expect and accept that. It is only later that the jury learns about the causation battle.

Here, we must transcend the arguments about law, rules, or liability. Defense attorneys are masters at the causation battle. They use exaggeration and hyperbole, like, "They are saying this good doctor, this family man who has worked hard all of his life to help people, maimed the plaintiff," or, "They are trying to say my client, this wonderful nurse, caused this horrific injury." We must show, rather than tell, the jury about how the carelessness directly caused the harm. We must also prepare them for this.

Modlin and Jones help me get experts. It can be difficult to separate experts who look great on paper but are not reliable as testifying witnesses from those who have the courage and verbal skills to match wits with opposing counsel. These trial consultants have seen hundreds of experts testify in front of juries and can thus provide a sound determination.

We are trained to deliver evidence and argue law. Trial consultants like Modlin and Jones watch hundreds of juries every year and have a better understanding of how we can try our cases like those which they have observed to be successful. We have to face up to the causation defenses. Part of this is framing issues the right way; another part is understanding the way jurors think about issues that arise in our cases—things like cancer, death, family, and hope.

Chapter 16

The Focus Group

There is no longer any doubt that pre-trial focus groups are the single most important device to prepare a case for trial. Much of the development of the jury science that Ball and Keenan write about in their indispensable books on damages and other topics is based on knowledge gained from years of listening to focus groups. The key value of focus groups is that the lawyer learns from a group similar to a jury what they think about the case before the trial actually begins. The lawyer can then form and plan the trial with input from the "jury."

At this juncture in the history of jury trial preparations, the question is not whether you should do a focus group, but what kind of focus group you should do in a particular case. The historic format is a mock trial, with at least 12 group members roughly similar to the demographic of the jurisdiction. The advantages of this format are that you get to simulate the trial, practice your arguments, and get feedback. The disadvantages are that 12 is an unwieldy number, unless you are dedicating an entire day to the process, and there is a real question of distortion because of the tendency to advocate harder for your side. The cost can also be an issue.

If the purpose is to evaluate whether you have a winner or need to settle the case before trial, a mock trial is valuable. If you are going to trial and your goal is learning about what jurors may be thinking about your case, the mock trial format is of less value due to the distortion your advocacy brings, because your unconscious desire to win, even at the focus group level, interferes with the process.

I now exclusively use what we call the "concept" (also known as "narrative") focus group, consisting of six to eight members, with some demographic distinctions of gender, age, and race. This option offers a relaxed format in which we allow the members to discuss the case collaboratively, after we give them a very brief rendition of the facts and answer questions for about a half hour.

My obsession with focus groups emerged many years ago through a former client who had worked for Procter & Gamble. This client was experienced in moderating focus groups for product testing. In these cases, we followed the model of mock trials, where I "represented" the client and my wife, also a trial lawyer, "represented" the opponent. We argued cases as a mix of opening statements and closing arguments, and then went behind a one-way glass to watch the focus group deliberate to a verdict. The cost of these focus groups was high, but we continued to do them when we or the clients could afford it. The mock trial model was good, but later I learned better ways to conduct groups to reduce the skewing.

Ball recommends in "Reptile" that the lawyer not be involved at all in the presentation or moderation of the focus group. I disagree. I think it is critical to be in the room and experience transference with the group as practice for creating transference at trial—something I can't do by watching the focus group on video later.

The concept focus group is the most relaxed forum for practicing your professional self-awareness in the use of transference as a trial tool. "Flirting," as the judge once accused me of doing, is a good way to think of this. If we can be "flirtatious" in a certain way with our focus group, we can probably use a similar manner with jurors in voir dire, our witnesses in direct examination, and even our opposing counsel in arguments in front of the jury. By opening this door to intimacy, we may be able to confirm our parental role and enhance our positive transference.

One of our focus group cases involved a catastrophic injury to Jim, a former college basketball player. When Jim was playing toss with young boys at a party to celebrate the opening of a newly built wooden deck, the deck rail split and collapsed, causing Jim to fall eight feet and break his neck.

One major difficulty in the case was that Jim had participated in building the deck with the homeowner, his brother-in-law. Another problem was that the homeowner had not gotten a building permit, which should have led to an inspection of the deck, including the failed connection. In our focus group, trial consultants Modlin and Jones worked on finding out what people thought about decks, wood, and building inspections.[29]

What we learned was that both men and women knew a great deal about carpentry and wooden decks. One of our participants pointed out that a lot of modern wood was "fast-grown" pine, which was treated very quickly to make it harder. He informed us that treated pine was wet and had to have some time to dry. Another person pointed out that the deck rail appeared to have been connected to the post at a right angle—the weakest possible connection. This information led us to further research into the source of the wood and the treatment process.

We were able to get the broken pieces of wood that some alert person had retrieved from the yard below. Based largely on the focus group's insight about the wood and connection, we hired a wood scientist to examine the wood itself. We discovered that the wood was not of the quality advertised. Thus, we now had a case about defective wood and false warranty, rather than poor construction. This was critical to success, as the group had agreed with the defense argument that Jim helped build the deck and, therefore, had personal responsibility.

This unavoidable fact was a very powerful "out" for the defendants, raising contributory negligence defense, which could destroy the case. As a result of the education we had received from the focus group on fast-dry wood, we sued the wood company, the company that manufactured the fastener, and the store where the homeowner had bought the wood. We not only found witnesses to establish that Jim had nothing to do with the construction of the deck rail or its fastening to the post, but also developed a theory that the wood was defective in quality and not the type advertised.

The case was settled at mediation for over $2 million. Jim was able to get a special wheelchair, a retrofitted van, and a computer that he could operate with his right index finger, which still had movement. Without the focus group, we probably would not have developed a case regarding the poor quality of the wood and would not have been so diligent in

29 One thing I have learned is to ask the focus group, rather than tell them, what the issues are. But in this first effort, I didn't yet know to do that. Still, simply by discussion, we learned what the group members thought.

showing that Jim had not worked on the deck railing that actually collapsed and caused the tragedy.

In this and other focus groups during that time period, we usually tried to have at least 12 members per group. We paid the members $50 and fed them dinner. If we could afford it, we rented a facility with a one-way mirror and videotaped the entire proceeding. This was expensive; our focus groups used to cost more than $5,000.

Now, we generally try to have only six- or eight-member panels, and we do them very informally. We find that a lower number allows for more discussion. It is also cheaper; we tend to spend no more than a couple thousand dollars.

Modlin and I start off explaining what the case is about in broad, general terms: "This case is about cancer. Write down 10 things you know about cancer." We then turn the discussion over to the members. We lead them gently toward important issues, but try to do so in the least intrusive way possible. We try to simply act as guides, not lawyers or leaders. The main function we supply is to make sure that one or two people don't dominate the discussion and that each member has some say.

I try to see how my comments or interaction affects my transference with the individuals in the group. I observe how the group reacts to the trial consultants. I listen. I watch.

In this way, we learn what is foremost in people's minds without filtering. We remove our own biases and ourselves from the process. Many times we don't even ask the members to decide the case, although sometimes we do so just to please our clients, who want to know the outcome.

Each case now presents an opportunity to analyze the unspoken dynamics of the upcoming trial. I am constantly trying to learn how to present a case from a psychodynamic level.

After every focus group, Jones reviews the videotape and the questionnaires and gives me a short outline of her thoughts. The most important part of what she does is to work with me on one-liners and analogies. In effect, we create the "rules of the road."

A lot of times, focus group members' comments become our one-liners at trial. The importance of one-liners is that they show gut feelings—the precursor to an intuitive connection between the case and a common or collective understanding of an evolved humanity. "Wood should be dry before it is sold." "The company put out a product knowing it was obsolete." "You shouldn't have to ask the doctor to give you a screening test." "You can only do what you can do." These are all examples of one-liners I have used in trials. One-liners can become rules or part of rules.

Analogies are also an important method of tapping into the unconscious. We often analogize a doctor's negligence to a driver's negligence in causing a car accident. I have analogized the BP oil spill to the failure of a doctor or hospital to review medical records. Analogies are important because they allow the jury to think more deeply on an unconscious level about the information they are receiving in a sometimes bewildering fashion. Analogies allow the jury to develop a gut feeling about the case.

An effective one-liner or analogy allows the jurors to organize the material of the trial according to their own experiences. This is similar to the Jungian theories of the evolved collective unconscious. One-liners and analogies are similar to myths and primordial thoughts, which Jung and his students studied a hundred years ago to show how our common humanity can be used to heal our neuroses.

Focus groups also give us rhetorical questions, which are not meant to be answered but are intended to make a salient point to an audience. Politicians use rhetorical questions such as, "Can we dare to be great?" or "How can we as a people let others suffer?"

Rhetorical questions in a trial can reach the issues in an unconscious and powerful way. "Ask yourself, would your doctor ignore you if you requested an ultrasound because you were worried about your baby's lack of movement?" "Would your doctor treat a patient like this doctor treated Ms. Smith?" "What kind of a company would fire a nurse for protecting the safety of a patient?" "Can you imagine a lifetime in a wheelchair, unable to walk to the refrigerator or go to the bathroom?"

Focus groups are the single most important method of educating oneself about how a jury may look at the case. With the information gained therein, we can gather the tools to awake our jury's intuition and persuade the jurors that what we are saying is true.

PART III

Dilemmas And Solutions

In Part III, you will find a number of common dilemmas lawyers face through the course of a jury trial. In each chapter, I will show how psychological methods can strengthen some of the more traditional strategies lawyers often use to solve these dilemmas.

Chapter 17

Dilemma: How to Get Good Jurors in Voir Dire

Solution: Attitude Toward Damages

During voir dire, we all have been trained to ask some version of this question: "If you feel the evidence has shown that Mrs. Client's injuries and harm were caused by the defendant's negligence, can you come back with a verdict for the plaintiff?"

Trial consultants started popping up at trial lawyer seminars in the 1980s. Many were social scientists who recognized that lawyers were poorly suited for jury selection; training in law school through the Socratic method and cross-examination led to close-ended questions to the prospective jurors and "dead juries." Often, lawyers would do all of the talking in voir dire. Although they felt they were impressing the jury and setting the stage for success in the trial, they were learning nothing about the jurors.

Trial consultants promoted the idea of asking prospective jurors open-ended questions to allow them to speak. Lawyers were to ask and follow up questions only, with no commentary or statements about the case. This was seen as a huge improvement; by finding out more about the jurors, lawyers widely felt that they were now better able to select those who would be more favorable to the plaintiff.

Over the years, a science of voir dire has developed based upon this idea of open-ended and follow-up questions.

The next area of voir dire science zoomed in on what to ask the jurors about. By attending numerous trials, jury consultants found that trial lawyers tended to shy away from asking jurors about things that were considered to be negative aspects of the case for the plaintiff or that the lawyers were worried about. The voir dire "scientists" began to focus on addressing the "bad stuff" up front, in voir dire, both as a defensive measure and to try to get jurors to either admit bias for cause or peremptory challenge or to get them to commit to understanding the problem and not letting it interfere with their ability to decide the case favorably toward the plaintiff.

Does this method of bringing out the bad and asking open-ended questions really get us better jurors? While very important and progressive, I believe it does not really face up to the harder part of psychodynamics of the jury's ultimate decision-making process to transfer money from the defendant's bank account to Mrs. Client's bank account.

So, how do we add psychodynamics to the science of voir dire to help us get better jurors and compensation for our clients?

In the past, I never thought that I should point-blank ask jurors if they are Republicans, agree with Republican principles of smaller government, or are afraid of things like the debt ceiling and China's purchases of our Treasury Bonds. However, I think the time has come when we can, and should, ask these questions.

Why? Because psychodynamics of the right—the Tea Party and even rank-and-file Republicans—dictate that any further transfers of wealth from the "wealthy" to the needy will destroy our American way of life. Because the brutal and honest truth about tort law is that at its most basic, the plaintiff is asking the jury to transfer wealth from the wealthy (doctors, corporations, insurance companies, etc.) to the needy, the injured, and the fired. Thus, what we are asking Republicans to do in the deliberation room is the antithesis of their political beliefs.

We cannot remove these jurors from our panels. Therefore, we need to take a different approach to see if such conservative prospective juror will be able to overcome his or her resistance to a plaintiff verdict. First, we have to recognize that behind the resistance is the psychological resistance to transferring wealth. So, how can we use psychodynamic and psychotherapeutic methods to overcome this deep resistance? In order to be successful, we have to identify and keep those conservative jurors who will ultimately be able to compromise.

Recall juror Gail, a very conservative Republican. In my interview with her, Gail remembered the judge telling the jury at the beginning of the trial that the plaintiff had been out on a dune buggy outside of town, from where he was taken to the emergency room following an accident. Gail was familiar with the dune buggy area, as many jurors are familiar with the hospitals, doctor groups, companies, and factories that we are suing in our tort cases. So, we need to find out about the juror's familiarity with the subject matter.

Gail had noticed people in the courtroom taking notes. They were not jurors. She immediately thought they must be jury experts. This made her feel more trapped. Why? Because she felt that she would be manipulated by jury consultants and lawyers. We need to keep consultants away from our table and ask them to be as discreet as possible.

Gail also remembered certain things about the voir dire. For example, the plaintiff's lawyer had asked everyone if they understood that his client was often ill and would have to leave the courtroom at times to go to the bathroom. We need to humanize our clients and not be scared of talking about them in the voir dire.

In fact, we should include some questions about the clients, in order to make our client a part of the voir dire experience so the conservative juror can develop empathy. "Ma'am, have you ever seen my client before?" "Does my client remind you of anyone you know?" In this way, we can begin to bring some transference into the courtroom. Even the most cynical and conservative people are subject to transference.

Gail recalled the plaintiff's lawyers being quiet and low key. They explained to jurors how difficult the trial would be. They told the jurors they appreciated the time the jurors were taking from their lives to come to the courtroom. They asked people if they could be fair, and if they could think of any reason for not being able to be fair. She told the lawyers that her daughter went to that dune buggy area with her friends; that didn't seem to bother anyone.

Gail likewise remembered the defense attorneys being "rude" to the jurors in voir dire. They said things like, "The plaintiff will 'try' to say…"—a verbiage she felt was insulting to the injured man and his wife. The sick lawyer wiped his nose on his coat sleeve as he questioned jurors, which she found "disgusting." We will not always be so lucky as to have rude and disgusting lawyers on the other side, but we do have to always control ourselves and be polite and distinguished.

What Gail didn't remember were a "bunch of details" about the case. As our jury scientists have been telling us for years, the attitude of the juror is more important than almost anything else. We do not need to waste time in voir dire asking about the facts of the case. That is what the trial is for.

When Gail was selected for the jury and found out that the trial would last up to a couple of months, she thought that was okay because she didn't work. However, the trial turned out to be very complicated and demanding, invoking the feelings of "isolation" and "pressure." Her main recollection of the opening statements was that the doctor had called in but didn't come in. This is the kind of fact that verdicts may hinge on for conservative jurors—not the medical details, but the breach of responsibility.

Let's not forget how hard it is to be a juror, and that it may be even harder for a juror to overcome a strongly held belief system against transferring wealth.

From Gail's experience, we see that even the conservative jurors are using their conscious and unconscious minds to evaluate what is in front of them. Before a word is spoken, they are able to look at the lawyers, the parties, the judge, and the other courtroom personnel and form a lasting opinion. They may have some information from the clerk about the case or the process in general, but at this point the appearance of counsel and parties has the most significance. Therefore, it is important to come across as neat, clean, and positive.

Voir dire is the only time in the trial when the lawyers can actually talk to and question jurors. This provides lawyers with an opportunity to use certain cues and bring up topics that will possibly cause jurors to begin the process of unconscious thought and intuitive thinking.

In this regard, it may be helpful to ask jurors about their childhood in a way that mimics the case before them. For example, if the case involves the death of a father by medical malpractice, the lawyer ought to ask jurors about their fathers—how important their father was to them, how the relationship continued throughout life, etc. This will cause jurors to begin the process of unconscious thought and transference, and may provide a basis for an intuitive belief that this case is about a father and how harm to a father has affected the rest of the family.

Voir dire is also an opportunity to attempt to cause transference to occur from at least some of the jurors to the lawyer. This can be done through the empathetic, gentle direction of free association to allow the jurors to connect current emotional feelings about persons and events to early childhood feelings about their parents or traumatic events. When speaking to a juror, the lawyer must, through nonverbal cues such as nodding and smiling, sincerely let the juror know that he understands in a positive way. These are the same psychodynamic methods that therapists use to overcome resistance.

Combining these therapeutic methods with the more scientific rigorous and disciplined questioning in an empathetic and open-ended manner will allow the juror to begin to experience the lawyer in the same way a patient experiences a therapist. The hope is that the lawyer can then lead the jurors to become more collaborative, with the therapeutic alliance opening them up and preparing them to work on tasks with the lawyer throughout the trial.

The lawyer should always allow the juror to speak openly and encourage the juror to trust him by always being empathetic with whatever the juror says, no matter how antithetical it may seem to the theory of the case. The Rogerian method of unconditional positive reinforcement is very helpful here. If the juror states he is Republican, ask what about the Republican Party that attracts him the most. Is it tax policy (transfer of wealth) or social issues? A "law and order" or "social issues" Republican might be better than one who feels overtaxed.

Achieving positive reinforcement in the therapeutic alliance can be done by engaging in "mirroring," or repeating what the juror has said. The lawyer can also "check back" with the juror by verbally making sure that the juror agrees with the goals and the task ahead. In any jury trial, the lawyer should first tell the jury that his goal is to find the truth for his client, that the juror's goal is to properly perform his civic function, and that the task to be worked on is the finding of truth.

We know that jurors are affected by advertising, political messaging, television, and the Internet. The most damaging messaging causes jurors to be suspicious of the legal system, believing that it is a lottery where fakers try to get rich at everyone else's expense and that lawyers are shysters only interested in a buck. As trial lawyers we are essentially playing

Robin Hood, trying to get money from the "wealthy" to the disadvantaged. It does no good for us to hide this under such phrases as the "legal system," or the "instructions of law."

Here, the work of Ball, Friedman, Keenan, and other lawyers/scholars can be very valuable in finding out which jurors have extremely strong beliefs that will cause them to oppose our case no matter what. I always use Ball's method of asking the juror a two-sided question, such as: "My sister believes that people get too much money in legal cases for pain and suffering, but my brother thinks that it is okay to give money for injuries like this. Are you a little closer to my sister or my brother?" This usually results in a very valuable discussion about money and pain and suffering, allowing me to identify and strike those jurors who are obviously biased and will be unlikely to award substantial damages.

One thing that we are trying to do is elicit an emotional response from the juror in voir dire, rather than a superficial conversation. Emotional responses are deeper and create unconscious connections.

Modern psychiatrists such as Sue Johnson recommend that the therapist create rifts and then repair them; the idea is to use emotional responses to treat the patient. To a degree, a lawyer can also use emotional response in voir dire to deepen the alliance with a juror and create a more positive transference. Only when we awaken the jurors' unconscious can we move toward our ultimate goal of jury persuasion.

Chapter 18

Dilemma: How to Weed Out Bad Prospective Jurors

Solution: Challenges

Beginning with consultants like Amy Singer and others in the 1980s, the strategy of using open-ended questions, followed by more open-ended questions, has become almost universally accepted as the proper method of voir dire.

The idea is that we need to determine a juror's "attitudes" toward issues important to the case in order to decide whether to keep her on the jury or find a way to strike her, either with a for cause or precious peremptory challenge. The way to find this out is to ask open-ended questions.

There are only two things a lawyer can hope to achieve in voir dire: first, to successfully find out who the worst three jurors are and strike them, and second, to begin a process akin to transference between the lawyer and the jury. How? By asking questions about childhood experiences with unconditional positive feedback, showing empathy, and being authentic and transparent—all core conditions urged by Carl Rogers in the therapeutic model of psychological counseling.

Sometimes things happen in voir dire that allow us to strike multiple jurors for cause. In an employment case I tried in federal court many years ago, representing a beautiful young woman who had been sexually harassed by her boss, I filed a motion in limine to keep the opposing counsel from bringing up anything regarding my client having had an abortion as a teenager.

The judge, a very strict and conservative man who was also a pro-life Catholic, granted the motion the day before trial and issued an order excluding the abortion from any part of the trial. The next morning, however, literally minutes before the beginning of voir dire, the judge changed his mind and said he would allow the evidence.

At that point I had a brainstorm: How could I use this unfair ruling to help me select a jury? This is how I conducted part of the voir dire:

> "Does anyone on this jury hold any opinion that abortion is wrong?" About six out of twelve raised their hands.
>
> "And of you six, how many believe that life begins at conception?" The same six raised their hands.
>
> "Sir, is it your opinion that a person who intentionally aborts a fetus is wrongful for taking a human life?"
>
> "Yes."
>
> "Those of you who believe that life begins at conception and who agree with juror number one, please raise your hand." The six pro-lifers raised their hands.
>
> "And sir, do you believe that a person who wrongfully takes a human life is in essence a murderer?"
>
> "Well, yes, I guess so."
>
> "Do you agree that under no circumstances would you be able to vote to award damages to a murderer in a case for damages?"
>
> "Yes."

I asked each one of the pro-life jurors this question. There was no way to rehabilitate these jurors. The judge was forced to grant my motion to strike them for cause. This probably allowed me to have the most liberal jury in the history of the District Court of the Southern District of Ohio. The result? A large verdict.

I have learned a lot about how to select juries, as well as thematic ways to try cases, from trial consultants Mark Modlin and Becky Jones. One of the most important elements to consider is how to handle peremptory challenges. Peremptory challenges are precious because we only get three in most jurisdictions in the country.

In a recent criminal trial in which I successfully defended a child psychiatrist who had been wrongfully accused of molesting five of his patients, I asked the jurors to tell me how they felt about psychiatrists. One juror, an older, unemployed lady, was loud, abrasive, and verbally abusive to me. She basically stated that she did not believe in psychiatry, and I got a bad feeling about her. I wanted to use a peremptory to strike her, but Modlin disagreed. "Don't strike her," he advised. "Save it for someone who may be influential in deliberations. No one will follow this lady. She will be a nonentity in deliberations."

It is of primary importance to strike, either by cause or peremptory challenge, prospective jurors who can never be persuaded, who will resist any transference, or who will have no chance of positive transference with the plaintiff or his lawyer. But if the juror is simply unpleasant, you might consider saving the peremptory for another juror who might have more influence.

The other important phenomenon that occurs in nearly every trial during voir dire is that, as shown in our concept focus groups, the jury will probably have the case almost entirely figured out in some fundamental way by the time voir dire ends. Thus, the opening statement is somewhat superfluous.

I now give very short openings, no more than 15 or 20 minutes, just to confirm what the jury already knows and to tell them what the case is about financially—what we expect and will ask for in damages. I also discuss the issue of wealth transfer. We should always explain that the transfer in this case is necessary, but that no more than is necessary should be awarded.

Chapter 19

Dilemma: How to Deal with Selective Memory

Solutions: Primacy and Recency

Most courts still do not allow jurors to take notes and are way behind in using technology to aid memory. The judge always instructs the jury that opening statements and closing arguments are not evidence. So, how can we as trial lawyers help jurors remember important testimony and highlight it so that it remains vivid at the end of the courtroom proceedings and in the deliberation room?

Another and sometimes greater problem is the weight that jurors ascribe to the testimony of eyewitnesses, many of whom may be defendants or associated with the defense. Elizabeth F. Loftus, professor of law and psychology at the University of California-Irvine School of Law, wrote an important book, "Eyewitness Testimony," on the topic in 1979.[30] The central thesis of this body of work is that eyewitness memory is not nearly as reliable as people think; Loftus presented multiple studies to prove this point. Criminal lawyers have long used the book to raise doubt about the testimony of eyewitnesses at criminal trials.

One section of this book relevant to civil trials is devoted to the idea of unconscious transference. Loftus discovered from her own experiments, as well as those of others, that when a group witnessed a crime, many of the group members identified a bystander they had seen close to the crime as the criminal himself. Loftus believed that many cases of mistaken identity could be caused by unconscious transference.

We need to recognize how a jury may unconsciously transfer an act from one person to another, mistakenly ascribing certain testimony to

30 E. F. Loftus. "Eyewitness Testimony," Harvard University Press, 1979.

the wrong witness. One way to prevent this is to discuss it at voir dire and opening, so that the importance of accuracy in recollection is one of the first things the jurors are told about. Another option is to quote verbatim portions of witness testimony from daily transcripts, or even our notes, in the closing.

Primacy and *recency* are well-studied concepts in psychology that address which presented information is best retained by the human brain. *Primacy* relates that people often remember best what they have heard first about a topic, continuing to give that first impression credence until or unless something later shows that this impression is wrong. Accordingly, we need to tell jurors things that we know to be true as soon as possible. If these things are negative to our case, we must explain them in a way that is consistent with how we intend to depict them later in the trial.

I used primacy effectively in one extremely difficult case, in which a nurse had been wrongfully arrested and we sued the hospital and security director for malicious prosecution. In order to win such a case, a lawyer has to prove more than a mistake by the defendant—he has to prove malice and that there were no reasonable grounds for the arrest and prosecution, which is very difficult to do. In this particular case, we had one fact that, if we could awaken the intuition of the jury, could lead to the conclusion that the security director had it out for the nurse.

The security director testified at his deposition that he recalled this nurse and a friend leaving his orientation lecture on the dangers of drug addiction in nursing before he had finished six years earlier.

In opening, I simply stated that the security director considered himself to be an expert in drug addiction in nursing; he gave an annual orientation to the nurses and considered this to be one of his most important duties as security director. Under the theory of primacy, we called him first, on cross, and fleshed it out, leading him into a discussion about drug abuse in nursing and how important this topic was to him, as well as his orientation class and how important it was to him.

I then asked him a series of questions:

"Mr. Jones, do you remember your drug abuse class in 1985?"

"Yes."

"Do you remember that T. C. was in that class?"

"Yes."

"Do you remember that T. C. left the class early?"

"Yes, she and a friend."

"You believe that it is important that the nurses attend your class, don't you?"

"Yes, because young nurses need to understand that they have access to dangerous drugs and can get addicted."

"And when you were investigating Ms. C, you remembered that she had left your class early, didn't you?"

"Yes."

We left it there, but through hinting, along with juror intuition that there may have been more than a mere professional interest, the jury knew from the beginning that the security director could have been predisposed against T.C. Ultimately, the jury found malice on this basis and awarded a million-dollar verdict. Afterward, the jurors told me that in deliberations they had agreed that the security director "had it in" for the nurse because she had left his class.[31]

Recency means that people tend to remember most clearly what they heard last on a subject—for example, just before leaving the courtroom after a day of work or for deliberations. That is why it is preferable to present damages charts and a complete discussion of the damages sought at the end of the trial.

I have learned that the thing jurors find most valuable is how to fill out the forms the right way, so I always blow up the verdict forms and actually fill out jury interrogatories with a magic marker in the rebuttal portion of the final argument. While most judges won't allow the jury to take the blowup back with them, it is worth it to ask. One judge actually did send my verdict form back on the theory that it would be helpful and avoid misunderstanding. Needless to say, that is my favorite judge.

The closing is also the time to show the hypocrisy of the other side and the inconsistencies in the evidence presented by the other side. Don

---

31 The lawyers are allowed to talk to jurors in state court in Ohio, but not in federal court. I always talk to the jury if I can, to find out whom they thought was the best or the worst witness and what they considered important. The jury then becomes a focus group for the future.

Keenan suggests that if you have a lie on the other side, "try the lie." In other words, make the lie the centerpiece of the trial. Under the principle of recency, make the lie the last thing you talk to the jury about in the rebuttal argument.

Chapter 20

Dilemma: How to Enhance Memory

Solution: Technology

We enhance the primacy phenomenon by focusing only on important issues and showing our most important documents or deposition transcript pages on a screen at the very beginning of the trial. We enhance the recency phenomenon by showing these things again when the opportunity arises, but always at the end of the trial. Recent advances in computer technology can help us do this in a strategic manner.

A Smart Board™ is a large computer and screen that is used in courtrooms across the country. It has many wonderful features and can be used by several different methods, including via a USB port or by simply plugging in a laptop. The upside to the Smart Board is that it is free and readily available. However, it is a huge object that is hard to maneuver. Many lawyers prefer to use projectors and screens or simply the "Elmo" to project.[32]

The important thing is to show the jury evidence and other items visually, not just tell them about these things. We know from focus groups and post-verdict interviews that jurors do remember documents and photographs that were blown up and shown repeatedly during the trial.

Trial Director, Sanction, and, to a lesser extent, PowerPoint are sophisticated and powerful presentation programs that allow the trial lawyer to organize trial exhibits and documents into folders and files, including synching depositions and video depositions, so they can be played for impeachment or when a witness is not available.

32 The "Elmo" is a projector that allows the lawyer to show individual transparencies. It is good when there is just a piece of paper that you want to show the jury or a witness.

PowerPoint comes with most laptop computers and can be effectively used in various ways. However, there are some limitations. PowerPoint as of yet does not allow us to synch video depositions with a transcript.

One of the most powerful presentation methods I have found is playing video clips snagged from YouTube or the Internet at large. In a recent trial, our claim was that a doctor had failed to properly screen our client for prostate cancer. As a result, by the time the patient found out he had cancer, it had metastasized to adjoining tissue and could not be surgically extracted simply by removing the prostate.

Defense experts testified that screening was no longer the standard of care; it was controversial because many prostate cancers were slow-growing and a patient could live a normal life and die of other causes without ever knowing he had prostate cancer. However, these expert urologists went even further. They insisted that the doctor had not violated the standard of care because my client *had not asked to be screened.*

The defendant doctor also testified at deposition that the standard of care required the patient to ask for screening, and since the patient had not asked for screening, he didn't offer it. This was a classic defense of appealing to the well-known value that people should have a sense of personal responsibility. I was troubled by this because our focus group had shown that this could be a potentially winning defense.

One evening while watching TV, I saw the Ally Bank commercial where a man was in a playroom with a young girl, sitting at a table. The man asked the girl if she liked horses. She said yes. He then asked if she would like a pony. She said yes. Finally, he pulled out a toy horse and gave it to her.

A young boy then came into the playroom and sat down at the table. The man asked the boy if he would like a horse, too. The boy said yes. The man brought out a *real* pony and gave it to the boy.

The little girl looked pained and said, "I didn't know I could get a real pony." The man sarcastically answered, "You didn't ask."

Then a voice-over narrated, "Even a child knows there are things you shouldn't have to ask for."

We snagged this popular ad and put it into our digital file. Playing this on a screen for the jury in the opening statement destroyed the main defense before the trial even started. The case settled for only slightly less than the demand in the second day of trial.

Chapter 21

Dilemma: How to Start

Solution: Brevity

One of David Ball's great contributions is his construction/deconstruction of the opening statement.[33] Ball's hypothesis is that the jury will believe the trial is about what you tell them it is about. The judge tells the jury upfront that the opening is not evidence and usually limits showing any documents or photographs as not yet in evidence. So, what is the best use of the opening statement? We follow what we have learned in focus groups and try to define the narrative, using the opening statement only to *define the case.*

We also have to discuss the fact that we are asking a jury not just to award damages, but to award them against the defendant, explaining why it is okay to transfer wealth in this instance. You may have to spend some time on this before the trial because, surprisingly, it is a difficult concept to explain. The introductory words, "The judge will tell you later in the trial…" may be helpful for allaying the jurors' rightful fear that they are going to be asked to take one person's hard-earned money and give it to another.

We have to acknowledge that this is an exception to the rule that every person has a God-given right to keep the fruits of his labor.

Ball's focus groups showed that there was a huge difference in jurors' attitude between an opening statement that focused on liability and

33 Ball has gone through an evolution on opening statements and now suggests certain exact phrases that he feels should be used. Whether you agree or disagree with these exact words, the idea that juries will believe that a trial is about what we tell them it is about is still a valuable lesson.

one that focused on damages. If he told a group, "This trial is about the question of whether a surgeon is liable for transecting the cystic duct or whether that is an acceptable complication of surgery," and later asked the group what the case was about, the group was more likely to say it was about a complication of surgery. However, if he told the focus group, "This trial is about the injury, loss, and harm a surgeon caused Mr. Smith when he cut something he shouldn't have cut," the group was more likely to convey later that the case was about the harm suffered by Mr. Smith.

What do you want the jury to think your case is about? Should you tell them up front that you are seeking a transfer from A to B of $1 million? Of course, the jury that has been told about the harm will be more open to a damages figure than the one that has been told about a technical, legal, or medical issue. Let the defendant's lawyer talk to the jury about liability. We need to talk about harm and damages because this is what we want the trial to be about. You can cover liability in voir dire, and then later in the trial.

You can address liability in summary fashion in the opening. For example, you might say something like this: "Obviously, the defendant denies he was at fault. We will prove to you in the trial through our witnesses that he was at fault and that his failure to act is undoubtedly the cause of the harm our client suffered." There is no need to go into any detail about the liability facts in opening.

Think about how your opening affects the unconscious transference between the jury and the lawyer as well. The statement on liability is bound to sound cold and technical to jurors, and most jurors are not educated in anatomy and surgery. They may not know what "transect" means, but they will certainly know what "loss of ability to get an erection" means. They may also hear "complication" as meaning "acceptable complication," unconsciously feeling that what happened is tragic but legally acceptable, as the defense will surely argue.

Thus, transference that naturally begins at the very first moment of the trial is nurtured and advanced favorably to the lawyer who appears paternally concerned about harm and remedies, rather than the one who is lecturing on things that are unfamiliar and technical. The intuitive instinct of the jury is that Mr. Smith has been hurt and the trial is about him getting compensation for the harm he suffered.

From our concept focus groups, we have learned that jurors know *before they step foot in the courtroom* that we are in a contest about liability. By the end of the voir dire, they also have a good idea of what the liability argument is about. We can use hinting and rhetorical questions to focus the jury on what is to come later, if we feel the information in the trial needs to be previewed.

Another thing we have learned from focus groups over the years is how much groups know about *everything*. The information is not always precisely correct, but it is surprising how much information about a variety of obscure topics focus groups know. A jury, as a similar group, therefore must be presumed to have vast knowledge about virtually all of the facts and issues in every case, even complex medical malpractice trials. Again, hinting is a relatively quick way to direct jurors in a subtle and succinct way, without insulting their intelligence by exhaustively going over all of the important issues again and again.

Don Keenan has discussed the importance of subtlety in opening statement in his blog. Some things are better left unsaid or half-said, he says, because invariably if we give jurors half of the information, they already know the other half or just need a little help putting the pieces together.

In "Reptile," Ball and Keenan recommend exciting the primitive part of the brain that acutely reacts to fear and survival—the "reptile brain"—to persuade each juror to view the trial from his or her personal point of view. The "reptile" perspective urged on jurors is to focus on how the harm experienced by the plaintiff relates to the danger a defense verdict may present to the jurors and their loved ones in the future.

This is entirely consistent with theories of the unconscious, as knowledge gained from the unconscious (i.e., intuition) is deeper and more persuasive than knowledge obtained simply by listening to the facts presented by the lawyer. Subtlety, therefore, like transference, is a way to encourage intuitive thinking on the part of the jury, which should be one of the main goals of the trial lawyer.

We are in the age of social networking, and lawyers are learning huge amounts of information about people, including their thoughts and attitudes, from Facebook and Twitter. This topic is worthy of an entire book, but the main lesson to be learned from Facebook and Twitter is that these social instruments have taught us about people's growing preference for brevity. People are now used to getting information in very brief sound bites. They then fill in the blanks with other acquired knowledge and intuition. Twitter is popular because it *requires* brevity, only transmitting up to 140 characters.

In response to this very real phenomenon and our knowledge from focus groups, we are trying to cut our opening statements to no more than 15 to 20 minutes. I have no doubt that as time goes on, my openings will be even shorter; we may be able to open in no more than 7 to 10 minutes, much of it accompanied by data electronically transmitted to jurors' handheld devices.

Information can be communicated more quickly than we previously thought because young jurors in particular likely know a lot more going in than we might have assumed in the past. The attention span of a normal 30-year-old is probably well less than 15 minutes and heading down. Jurors are used to multitasking—watching TV, texting friends, checking emails and the weather, and getting scores of the games, all at the same time.

I envision that I will give the following opening statement in a case that will be tried later this year:

Ladies and gentlemen, a nurse holds a special place in our emergency rooms. She must quickly and expertly figure out which patients are more acutely ill and need more attention. For example, she has rules that all nurses must follow when a patient has expressed a suicidal plan (show the ER suicide policy on the screen).

These rules protect the safety of all patients.

The judge will tell you later in the trial that a nurse may not be fired because she had followed these rules and protected the safety of her patients.

The defense will try to convince you that Lindsey was fired because she had disobeyed her supervisor's instruction to interrupt her care of a suicidal patient. But, the whims of a supervisor cannot overrule the standard set by hospital guidelines and policies. It is not insubordination to follow the accepted rules.

Lindsey followed the rules, but the hospital broke its rules by firing her. Because the supervisor broke the patient safety rule and fired Lindsey, she has suffered great harm. She has lost her job and was humiliated in front of her peers. She is fearful of returning to work as a nurse.

Although a verdict for Lindsey will require the transfer of money to her from the hospital, it is not some type of entitlement like we have in government. This is strictly a private enterprise—compensation like an employer pays an employee—just a different kind of free-market enterprise.

We will, therefore, ask you at the end of the trial to reaffirm by your verdict that a nurse's first duty is to protect the safety of her patient, and that the hospital cannot force her out of her job without paying for it.

Thank you.

This two-minute opening tells the whole story without any specific facts. Anything more would be superfluous. We have defined the case.

Chapter 22

Dilemma: How to Address a Powerful Defense Opening

Solution: Impeach the Opposing Counsel

What if we have presented a very brief and effective opening statement, but then the defense counsel delivers a powerful but exaggerated opening that is very damaging?

The injured persons have to put on their case in chief first. Because our opening for them is so brief, we should first call a witness who has important and specific information about the rules and the theme presented in the opening. This advances the primacy phenomenon and reconfirms the subtle message we have just given the jury. It also brings the jury back to our case from the opening of the defense that the jury has just heard.

There are as many theories on what witness to put on first as there are plaintiff lawyers, but I like to select either the defendant or a defense witness who knows a lot about the case. Cross-examining him or her with leading questions allows me to tell the story I want to tell. I always ask the judge whether he permits the defense attorney to ask questions after my cross or whether that counsel has to wait until the defense case in chief to direct her client or witness. If the judge allows immediate re-direct—and, therefore, immediate rehabilitation—I start with another witness.

The idea here is to give the opening statement on liability through a witness, rather than in the opening itself. This is a way to make the theory of negligence more credible. It's okay to tell the jury that you will be leading the witness *for the sake of saving time*. This is done by telling the witness:

> "Mr. Smith, I am going to ask you questions that will require you to agree with a "yes" or disagree with a "no." Of course, if you feel you need to briefly explain your answer, you should do so, but not until you have affirmatively or negatively answered the question. Is that okay?"

The defendant must be handled with great care. He obviously wants to tell the story his way, not our way, and may try to disrupt the leading questions. You can't let him do that. If he starts pontificating, gently interrupt. If the defense objects, ask the judge to remind the witness to answer the question as asked. Ask the defendant if he is willing to answer your questions. If he says no, ask the judge to tell him to answer the questions.

One way to quickly get the jury on your side is to pit the opposing party against his own lawyer, a method pioneered by renowned trial lawyer Richard Lawrence in the 1990s. This is often available as a tool if the opponent lawyer bends the facts in the defense. Trial consultant Mark Modlin and I have successfully used this method in a recent medical malpractice trial.

The defendant was a family doctor, whose very experienced and excellent lawyer had taken the position from day one that once his client had sent the patient to a specialist, under the standard of care he was no longer responsible for the failure to screen for cancer. We had settled with the hospital and the specialist before the trial began.

My opening was longer than it should have been, but I did set out a rule that a doctor who sends a patient to the lab for testing has a continuing duty to inform the patient and take action if the lab result turns out to be abnormal. The family doctor had broken this rule.

In his brilliant and adversarial opening statement, lasting at least 45 minutes, the defense lawyer skewered this rule in the following manner:

> "What Mr. Whitman fails to tell you is that my client had sent the plaintiff to a specialist. He fails to tell you that experts agree that once the family doctor sends a patient to a specialist, he is entitled to rely on the specialist to screen and test. Mr. Whitman fails to tell you that my client is not an expert in cancer, and the standard of care for a family physician does not require him to conduct annual screenings. So, I urge each of you jurors to ask yourselves the question throughout this trial:
>
> 'Why is Dr. Smith here? I repeat, 'Why is he here in this courtroom?'"

The problem for the defendant? His office notes showed that he had continued to screen for cancer, but erratically, and that he never told the specialist or the patient that one of the patient's PSA prostate cancer screening tests had been abnormal. No one other than the family doctor knew! With this record, the defendant could hardly take the position that he was not subject to the rule exactly as I had stated it.

So, my questioning of the defendant went like this:

"Doctor, you have heard your lawyer give a brilliant opening statement, haven't you?" He had to agree.

"And, doctor, is it true that there is such a thing in medicine called 'co-managing?'" He had to agree.

"You were co-managing my client's cancer screening at least twice by sending him to the lab and ordering the PSA screening on this request form (show the form with the PSA box checked), right?"

The defense attorney jumped up, "Objection, can we approach, Your Honor?"

Now I had the jury's rapt attention. I also had the defense attorney's rapt attention. He asked the judge to strike the question as "assuming facts not in evidence."

The judge told me to restate, so I did:

"Doctor, did you hear the opening statements?"

"Yes."

"Isn't it a fact that your lawyer told the jury that you were not legally responsible for cancer testing because you had sent my client to a specialist?"

"Objection," bellowed the defense lawyer, "move to strike."

"Overruled," said the judge.

"What was the question? I didn't understand it," asked the doctor.

At this point, we were gaining valuable points into the unconscious and intuition of the jury. The defense was trying to avoid answering an easy question.

I asked the court reporter to repeat the question.

"Yes, that is what he said," said the doctor.

"Doctor, is co-managing an acceptable and standard practice in medicine?"

"Yes."

"And when you co-manage a patient, you have continued responsibility for the patient, right?"

"Yes," he agreed, "but only for the part I am co-managing. I am not a cancer specialist."

"For example, in your practice you often co-manage cancer patients receiving chemotherapy, orthopedic patients who need post-operative care, and many other situations, don't you?" He had to agree. The jury already knew it to be true from their own experiences anyway, so he couldn't deny it.

"Let's look at your chart again, doctor." I put the digitized chart up on the Smart Board. It showed that he had lab results in the chart. The lab result in one instance was abnormally high, clearly marked with a bold capital **(H)**.

The defense lawyer objected that the chart had not yet been submitted or accepted by the court as an exhibit, but this fell on deaf ears with the judge, who reminded counsel that there was a stipulation as to the doctor's certified chart and explained to the jury that a stipulation meant that the parties had agreed the documents were admitted into evidence. This was another unconscious point for our side, prompting the jury to intuitively infer that the defense was hiding something from them.

"Isn't it true that you were aware that my client was seeing the specialist at the time that you ordered cancer screenings by the lab and got the results?" The doctor had to agree, as he had already admitted he had referred the client to the specialist earlier.

"Doesn't your own chart show that you were, at these several times when you got labs and asked for cancer screening, at least during these occasions, co-managing the patient with the specialist?" Now the doctor was in a box. He had to agree.

"So, when your lawyer told this jury no more than an hour ago that once you had referred the client to the specialist you no longer had responsibility for his cancer screening, that was not true, was it?'

"Objection, the doctor said he was only responsible for the part he was doing," called out the defense counsel.

"Overruled," said the judge. "Doctor, you may answer."

"I am only responsible for the part I am co-managing," the doctor replied, mimicking his lawyer.

"But, doctor, you just testified that you sent the patient for cancer screening twice and once the result came back abnormal, didn't you?" He had to agree.

"And so, you were responsible for co-managing the abnormal screening you found, right?" He had to agree.

"And there is no indication that you sent the abnormal lab to the specialist in your file, is there?"

"No. There is no fax copy, as I told you in my deposition."

"So, your lawyer was wrong when he told this jury that you were not legally responsible because you had sent the patient to a specialist, isn't that true?"

"I guess so," the doctor replied reluctantly.

"Your lawyer told the jury that they needed to ask themselves the question, 'Why is this family doctor here?' throughout the trial."

"Yes, I heard that."

"Isn't your co-managing the patient the answer to that question? Isn't that why you are here?"

The doctor looked at me, the jury looked at the doctor, the defense attorney looked at his papers, and I looked at the jury. Precious moments went by as the jury waited for the answer they already knew.

"Yes," the doctor said quietly.

Modlin and I discussed this afterward. We agree that if it is at all possible, especially when opposing counsel has given a great opening, the trial lawyer should try to separate that counsel from the defendant by showing the jury, as soon as possible, that the defense lawyer's opening statement was overstated in some way. This is *polarizing* at the most elemental level, and it creates a terrible unconscious feeling about the defense.[34]

---

34 "Polarizing" is a concept that Rick Friedman has written a book about, "Polarizing the Case." Very briefly, in polarizing the case you want to force the other side to take the most extreme positions possible, so that you can then, through solid evidence, rebut those extreme claims.

Of course, the defendant might be formidable and make his own case during the cross-examination. However, the ability to use leading questions allows us to set the stage for the rest of the trial. Even if the defendant is a great witness for herself and won't agree to the facts presented in the leading questions, the story gets through.

The benefit of calling a defense witness first, and if possible pitting the witness against the defense lawyer, in my opinion, is almost always worth the risk. The idea is that, by using the defendant as a foil through the power of leading questions, we get to *frame the case* the way we want it framed through the defendant. Other witnesses can also be used as foils this way in order to frame the case.

Framing the case is a way to set a theme, which then can be used throughout the trial. In the case above, we framed the case as negligent co-management that led to a too-late discovery of cancer. Everything relevant to liability and causation that we presented from that point on emphasized this theme, from the testimony of our client and his wife to that of the experts in family medicine and oncology.

By this early framing, we let the jury know what we thought the trial was about with respect to liability. The trial became very simple from that point on, as we could focus primarily on the harm caused. Each witness reiterated how the late discovery of cancer had affected our client and his family, and the trial was now played on our terms. Thus, we were able to overcome a big barrier in chief by framing the issue.

In this case, we didn't even have to get to damages or a verdict—the defense settled the case for the demand before they even put on any witnesses.

There is another way to frame: the very simple, but effective method of raising your voice at important times. When there is one factor or issue that I feel is primary to point out the hypocrisy of a defense witness, I will quite intentionally raise my voice, as though angry to question the witness about this. I then repeat raising my voice every time I address this issue.

This works for me because I am generally pretty low-key and friendly, even to difficult and obnoxious defense witnesses. It might not work as well for lawyers who already use a lot of heat or volume in the way they talk or question witnesses.

I used this strategy in my two-month pitched battle with the Justice Department in the federal conspiracy criminal jury trial discussed earlier. My client was one of the executives charged with conspiracy to commit bank fraud, wire fraud, credit card fraud, and mail fraud. A key point in the conspiracy was a meeting that had taken place where the conspirators had allegedly planned how to defraud customers and banks.

The government had made a deal with one of the top executives of the company, allowing her to plead to a lesser offense in exchange for her testimony against her former colleagues. One of the key points of her testimony was a description of this seminal meeting. I knew that my client had not been in the country on the date of this meeting. He had been in India, and I had passport information to prove it.

This witness was desperate to please the government and went after all of the defendants, including my client, with a vengeance. She testified that my client "to the best of her memory" was at this meeting and had participated in planning the scheme.

In an eight-week trial, details and facts tend to get jumbled up and lost in the voluminous and complex body of evidence. I knew that on cross-examination I could either get the witness to recant or call my client a liar; however, in order to polarize the case, I needed a way to let the jury know that this was a critical point in the plethora of facts.

So, I quietly went about the cross-examination until I got to the meeting. Then I raised my voice a lot, so that instead of the quiet, affirming lawyer the jury had learned to expect and project as the caring parent, I was suddenly an angry father who had caught the child in a lie:

> "So, is it your firm testimony that [my client] was at the meeting at corporate offices when these business procedures were created and put into place?"
>
> "Yes, to best of my memory."
>
> "And it is this meeting and his participation in this meeting that led you to believe he was a knowing participant in this conspiracy?"
>
> "Yes, partially."
>
> "If [my client] says he wasn't at this meeting, would you agree with him?"
>
> "No, because I remember him being there."

"So, if my client says he wasn't even in the country, are you saying he is a liar?" Now my voice reached high decibels. The jury focused. The government attorneys frantically shuffled papers. I proceeded with polarizing, clearly feeling the heightened tension in the courtroom. I knew that the jury would remember this moment.

At final argument I was brief about this issue. When I discussed it, I told the jury: "Remember, there was only one time I got angry and raised my voice. I did that because the prosecution was wrong. I put the passport stamp and immigration papers on the screen. It was clear that my client had not been at this critical meeting. Please don't ruin the life of this wonderful young man. Please, please find him not guilty."

And they did.

Chapter 23

Dilemma: How to Deal with Defense Experts

Solution: The "What" Question Strategy

Expert witnesses can be a huge thorn in our side in a medical malpractice, product liability, or even a simple slip-and-fall or car wreck case. As trial lawyers, all of us have had problems with our experts and ensuring that they support our case at trial.

I always tell my experts that there is one rule that is non-negotiable: Once we have agreed on the extent that they can support our theory of the case, they must always, at deposition and trial, support the theory with their opinions 100 percent. There can be no backing down, no equivocation, and no modification. If they are uncomfortable with any aspect of the theory of the case, we must discuss it and make a decision before the deposition (or written report, as required in federal court). Once decided, there can be no changes. I back this up with an email with bullet points and a subject line titled "your opinions," reiterating that there can be no "misunderstandings," no "realization" while under cross-examination.

Opposing experts present a host of problems. Some of these experts simply testify that the arguments of the plaintiff are wrong or arguable on basic science. Others pose alternative theories of the cause of injury. Others still deny that there was any harm at all. Almost all of them deny that the harm or the extent claimed was caused by the defendant.

How to conduct the cross-examination of defense experts is one of the most studied and published areas of trial law. Dorothy Sims teaches courses all over the country on how to cross-examine a doctor hired by the defense to conduct an independent medical examination of the plaintiff. Professor James McElheny has written several books and numerous articles dedicated to this important and difficult aspect of the trial.

One of the recent ideas in this area has arisen from an unknown source,[35] and it is one I have found to be very effective in focus groups. It is called the "what questions" strategy. This method entails asking experts questions that they will not be prepared to answer, but that have relevance to the expert opinion from a layperson's perspective and intuition.

One thing that focus groups show, but lawyers have long ignored, is that jurors expect experts to know a lot more about the particular case and the parties involved than they actually do. By this, I don't mean the medicine or science of the case, but the factual information about the parties involved.

We usually ask the defense expert witness what he has reviewed, finding that he has reviewed the medical records and the depositions of other witnesses. Usually by this time in the proceedings, he has been paid at least a couple of thousand dollars, and often much more. But invariably, the defense expert has not carefully read the CV of the defendant, has never seen the office or hospital where the defendant works, has no idea who the defendant's partners are or what kind of group he works with, and has no personal data about the defendant gathered from the Internet or other resources. Jurors expect that an expert witness paid this kind of money would know all of the facts, not just the narrow foundation underlying his or her opinions.

As jurors have very high expectations of experts, one important course of cross-examination suggested on the trial lawyer list serve was to ask the expert witness questions that are very open-ended, rather than leading. These are called "what questions."

A great example of this would be to ask the expert nothing at all about the plaintiff, but a lot of "what questions" about the defendant, the other defense experts, and even the defense lawyer. These questions can be about anything that we think the expert should know before rendering opinions in a case, even about the city and state where the case is being tried (experts are usually from out of town).

35 Trial lawyers use listserves to weigh in on various topics. This is one that I came across several years ago. I don't know who started the string, but whoever created it should be recognized as a brilliant legal thinker.

This can be a very important strategic maneuver, especially if the juror has already acquired some intuitive sense from your early impeachment of the defendant, by leading questions, that the defense attorney may be exaggerating the facts. Showing that opposing counsel's very expensive expert really doesn't know a lot about the case can help impeach the expert's credibility. Unconsciously, the jurors are processing and deciding. The more we can do to create doubt about the other side, the better chance we will have.

So, how can we do it? First, set it up by having the expert acknowledge that she was hired by the defense attorney to address the conduct of the defendant, and that she was provided very voluminous records. Emphasize the many thousands of dollars she has likely received for the review of the documents and every aspect of the case. The expert will have to admit that it is important to learn about the entire picture of the case in order to testify credibly. Use the language of the jury instruction on expert testimony that the purpose of expert testimony is to help the jury evaluate "similar facts and circumstances."

Now start asking questions the expert never expected to be asked—not about your client, literature, or his experience and training, but about the defendant, the defense experts, or the defense attorney.

For example:

"What is the type of practice the defendant doctor is engaged in?"

"He is a family practitioner."

"What is the normal number of patients the defendant doctor sees daily?"

"I don't know."

"How many patients did the defendant doctor see on the day he saw the plaintiff?"

"I don't know."

"What testing facility does the defendant doctor have available in his office?"

"I don't know."

"What staff did the defendant doctor have working in the office the day the plaintiff was there for his annual physical examination?"

"I don't know."

Or something like this:

"You were hired by Ms. Defense Attorney, were you not?"

"Yes."

"And you have worked with her and her law firm in the past, correct?"

"Yes, several times."

"What kind of cases does Ms. Defense Attorney generally work on?"

"I don't know."

Or this:

"What does Dr. Jones, the other expert testifying for the defendant, specialize in?"

"I think urology."

"How many doctors are there in his group?"

"I have no idea."

"So you don't know if he has had an opportunity to discuss this case with his colleagues?"

"No."

"And you have never discussed this case with the other expert, have you?"

"No."

"What is the basis for the other expert's opinion in this case?"

"I don't know."

The psychodynamic tool we need to use here is resistance—not resistance to our case or theory, but to an "expert" who is not familiar to the case. We take what we know to be a powerful unconscious force (resistance) and instead of trying to overcome it, work to foster it.

In essence, we are narrowing down the knowledge of the experts, for whom the jury has very high expectations. I heartily recommend that in each cross-examination of a defense expert, a portion or even all of it be dedicated to the "what questions" modality. It doesn't solve the problem of good opposing experts, but to the extent that it sheds some doubt, it works.

Chapter 24

Dilemma: How to Address the Burden of Proof

Solution: Polarizing and the "Burden of Proof" Jury Instruction

I believe the single greatest impediment to a successful and fair decision by the jury is the jury instruction that says the plaintiff has the "burden of proof," which can only be sustained by a "preponderance of evidence." Beyond the obvious problem that these are obtuse and abstract concepts that people never use in their real lives, how to neutralize this damaging instruction is the primary duty of the plaintiff trial lawyer.

"Polarizing the case" is an important concept in this battle, as it distinguishes the plaintiff case or witness from the defense. It is counterintuitive in the sense that we usually try to keep severe criticism of our clients at a minimum, but here we emphasize the most extreme criticisms of our client by opposing counsel and ridicule them as exaggerated. Polarizing is a theory that says you should invite criticism, particularly unfair criticism. This takes some planning and some skill, because what you are doing is essentially tricking the defense into taking more extreme positions than they should.

The concept of polarizing the trial is the brilliant creation of Rick Friedman, a primary modern lawyer-scholar of how to try jury trials.[36] To follow his method, we start with the premise that people are oriented toward respect for rules much more than the more vague "standard of care" or what a "reasonable person would or would not do under the circumstances."

Breaking a rule is clear; departing from a standard of care is vague. Why our jury instructions are so vague and ambiguous is a mystery, but

36 R. Friedman. "Polarizing the Case," Trial Guides, 2008.

Friedman advises changing the language for clarity. This makes the jury more comfortable with the legal concepts of liability and causation.

The next step, after clarifying the rules, is to polarize the case, never letting the defense get away with insidious innuendos about our client, such as malingering, greed, honesty, motivations, etc. For example, when a defense doctor gets on the stand and talks about "secondary gain," with the underlying but unspoken message that our client is a fraud just looking for free money, we have to get the underlying message out on the table in a clear and unambiguous way, make the expert define "secondary gain," and then say, "Oh, you mean my client is a liar?"

This is counterintuitive, but don't be scared to get it out on the table. Of course, a scheming client is a losing client, so we trial lawyers have developed a habit of glossing over or explaining the bad things about our clients, with hope that the jury would forget or overlook the innuendo. But juries don't forget.

By addressing the innuendo directly and making the witness overstate or make an outrageous allegation against our client that obviously is not true, we can overcome the insidious innuendo. Once we let them state the outrageous allegation against our client, we can then produce witnesses to show that our client is not a fraud. Jurors intuitively feel that plaintiffs who have families, jobs, and friends willing to stand up for them are not liars.

This is, of course, a way of activating the unconscious of the jury, of activating transference from the jury to the client, so that the jury sees the client as a victim twice—first as a victim of the tortfeasor and now of the defense. Polarizing should be set up from the beginning of the trial, enabling jurors to unconsciously relate the experience to their own childhood memories of adult figures dismissing them.

Once the defendant has asserted that our client is a liar and a schemer, we have set up a burden of proof for the defense to prove. Here is where we can use a forgotten jury instruction to our benefit. Even though the universal jury instruction states that the burden of proof is that of the plaintiff by a preponderance of evidence, every set of jury instructions I have seen has one that begins this way: "A party who asserts that certain facts exist must produce evidence to prove those facts. This is called the burden of proof."

This instruction applies to *both* parties, so we can use it to argue to the jury that while the defendants asserted that our clients are liars, frauds, and malingerers, they did not carry the burden of proof.

Here is how we can address this in the final argument:

It's very simple, ladies and gentlemen: We carried our burden of proof. We proved carelessness, departure from the established rules, and that this caused harm and injury.

The defendants, on the other hand, did not carry their burden of proof that my client is a liar, a malingerer, and a fraud. They cannot be allowed to get away with this, ladies and gentlemen.

The judge will tell you that they must prove what they assert. That is the only burden the defense carries in a trial. They failed and, therefore, their defense has failed.

Chapter 25

Dilemma: How to Emphasize

Solutions: Pointing, Props, and Introducing

After leaving a firm as a young lawyer, I hung up my shingle, hit the streets, and tried more than 30 public defender criminal jury trials.[37] I soon recognized that invariably the prosecutors always pointed at my client when a police officer or eyewitness identified him or her. I wondered why they did that.

Figuring that it might work for me as well, I later started to point at the defendants in my civil trials. I now know that pointing the index finger at someone is a very powerful nonverbal tool. It is accusatory. It is damning. It is very powerful.

Another potent gesture is making a fist and punching. I learned this from a prosecutor as well, one of my most important opponents, who is now an appellate judge.

Some years ago, I was hired to defend a young 20-year-old man, an heir to a large family fortune who had gone to a special high school called the School for the Creative and Performing Arts (SCPA). He was an actor. His parents had divorced when he was young, and his wealthy father now lived in Los Angeles with a second family. His mother had cared for him, but descended into drugs and a life of poverty.

37 I still love criminal trials because not only is there so much at stake, but there is also little or no discovery. Cases are tried on the floor of the courtroom, so skills like using transference and projection, unconditional positive regard, and other therapeutic methods are even more important than in some of the civil cases.

This handsome and charming young man was charged with murdering his infant son by striking him in the abdomen to stop him from crying, and then disposing of his body in a woody area near his girlfriend's apartment. When questioned by police, he had at first denied knowing anything about the missing boy. Several days later, however, he admitted that he had lightly punched the boy to stop his incessant crying. He denied any intent of harming the boy.

To add to the difficulty, my client was white, aristocratic-looking, and married to a beautiful young woman of mixed white and black race, while his girlfriend was an 18-year-old, lower-income African-American—attractive, but not educated. In my part of the country in the early 1980s, this was not an acceptable picture to most jurors.

I tried that case against two young prosecutors, who have remained my friends, colleagues, and respected adversaries. I knew by then that at some point one of them was going to dramatically turn and point his finger at my client at a crucial point in the trial. But one went a step further—and taught me a lesson I will always remember.

My client testified that he had been asleep and the baby woke him up. The infant wouldn't stop crying, so my client lightly tapped him in the stomach to see if that would stop him from crying.

The prosecutor picked up a doll from a bag at his table and approached my client:

"So you were in bed next to the baby, your son?"

"Yes."

"And you tried to make him stop crying?"

"Yes."

"So you *punched* the baby like this?"

The prosecutor punched the doll in the stomach.

My client looked at him.

"Yes," he said quietly.

I now always try to use some kind of a prop to show the jury. I have shown jurors surgical towels and beer bottles, pieces of deteriorated wood and medicine bottles, maps of railroad yards and seat belts. Demonstrations work because they are genuine and transparent. They create an atmosphere friendly to transference and intuition and encourage a developing alliance.

Another brilliant idea I have learned from a defense attorney specializing in medical malpractice cases is the simple act of putting up one or more pictures of your key witnesses on a screen in the opening statement.

What does this do? First, under primacy principles, the jury will tend to find these witnesses more credible simply because they saw them early in the trial. When these witnesses walk into the courtroom, the jury will be familiar with their faces. Second, this creates a sense of transparency. Third, it enables the jury to begin an intuitive process about each one of the witnesses before they start their testimony.

For the same reasons, I would not recommend showing photographs of the defense witnesses or experts.

Showing photographs in the opening is one way of *introducing* each topic of examination for each witness. This can then help jurors in direct examinations and cross-examinations.

Introducing a topic when questioning a witness lets you inform the jury of what's to come. For example, you might say to your medical expert, "Doctor, I am now going to ask you about the visits my client had to your office from August 1, 2008, to August 1, 2009, okay?" This introduces the topic to the jury and is in line with the congruence principle of transparency, which is an important aspect of positive transference we are seeking to engender

Once you have finished with the topic, introduce the next one, like this:

> "Doctor, have we discussed all of the office visits between August 1, 2008, and August 1, 2009?"
>
> "Yes."
>
> "Okay, now can we move our attention to how these visits are important, in your opinion, in relation to [my client] suffering a permanent injury in this accident?"

This mix of *introducing* and then *framing* is something I try to do with all witnesses, especially expert ones. Expert witnesses are trying to provide information with authority and are essentially working from an outline, which should look something like this:

1. Qualifications: "Doctor, let's first address your education and training, so that the jury understands why you are qualified to give your opinions in this case. Is that okay?"
2. Negligence: "Doctor, now let's turn our attention to why the defendant departed from the standard of care of a careful and prudent doctor. I have some questions for you about that."
3. Directly and proximately caused: "Doctor, have we discussed the departure from the standard of care sufficiently? Okay, let me now ask you some questions directed at how this doctor directly and proximately caused my client to suffer. Are you prepared to discuss this?"
4. Harm, injury, and loss: "Doctor, have you and I discussed how the defendant's departure from the standard of care directly and proximately caused harm to the plaintiff? Are there any other ways? No? Now I would like to ask you some final questions focused on the harm, injury, and loss that was caused."

After introducing a topic, it is important to stick to what you promised to address. If you tell the jury you are going to ask questions about the day of the accident, don't move away from it until you have introduced the next topic. Remember, what we are trying to do is create and nurture jurors' transference and intuition. We can't afford to confuse them with jumbles of questions. We should make it easy for their unconscious to focus on what we want it to focus on.

By introducing the topics in this order, we are helping the jury transparently see what the witness is trying to communicate. Introducing adds authenticity. Transparency and authenticity are part of the methods urged by Carl Rogers in the congruence of therapist and patient.

From the psychodynamic perspective, we should always be seeking to be genuine, transparent, and authentic. Introducing, like subtlety at the other end of the spectrum, is an important way of communicating to the individual and collective unconscious of the jurors that we are empathetic and positive. Introducing is a juror-centered strategy.

When we try the case for the jurors, and not for our own benefit, we are more likely to succeed. Then, when we ask them to take Peter's money to pay Paul, we have placed ourselves in a position of trust. Without this trust, there is no way a jury will ever take someone else's money away and give it to another person.

Here's another important point: Our focus groups have shown that jurors are very well aware that lawyers get a percentage of the damages. How likely are they to give the defendant's money to the plaintiff if they don't like or trust us? Not very.

Chapter 26

Dilemma: How to Persuade

Solution: Arming to Encourage Intuition

The trial is almost over. All of the witnesses have been called and questioned. We have done our best to frame, polarize, and use transference and projection. Now, we have to stand up in front of the jurors and talk to them directly.

We know from Freud, Jung, Rogers, and other scholars that as well as we may try a case, and as well as we may direct the jury to consider certain evidence, there are other forces at work in the courtroom that affect jurors.

In most cases, there are going to be jurors who are very receptive and favorable to our side, those who are less favorable, and possibly some who favor the other side. Once the trial moves into deliberations, only our unconscious influence survives in the jury room. Thus, the final argument is our last chance to win the case verbally.

How can we continue to exert some influence over the jurors after they leave the courtroom and are sequestered in the jury room to decide the case?

David Ball recommends arguing the case to those jurors who will be your advocates and urging them to use your arguments in deliberations in debating the case with fellow jurors. He calls this "arming" the jurors who are going to favor your side during deliberations. This promotes an alliance that is similar to the therapeutic alliance and helps achieve a positive transference.

"Arming" means telling (or asking) the jurors who are on your side, or have had a positive transference psychologically with you and your client, to use your arguments in the jury room when faced with counter-arguments. It means making sure these favorable jurors understand what jury instructions are important, what these instructions mean, and how to best explain them to other jurors if there is a dispute. It also means giving jurors the facts by reiterating testimony and showing important exhibits on the screen one last time during the final argument, specifying which exhibit numbers will support your side.

On the unconscious level, by arming the jurors with confirmatory facts, you also continue to further your positive transference with those jurors. Tell the jury in the final argument that you *expect* that the jurors who support the plaintiff will speak up in deliberations, that they cannot allow other jurors to pollute deliberations by bringing in external issues, and that they can ask the judge to intervene, if necessary, if deliberations are not on point. As we have learned, groups tend to follow certain paths. We need to tell jurors this and remind them that if things break down, the process may not be fair.

Another powerful unconscious tool that can be used in the final argument is music. Music is the universal language, so why not use it? I have asked the jury to "light my fire," told them that my client who had to work despite being in pain was "back on the chain gang," reminded them that a family is a "circle filled with love," and comforted them with, "Don't think twice, it's all right."

I believe that our common experiences and collective unconscious can be powerfully influenced by familiar song titles or lyrics that fit the case. One of our past lions of the bar in Ohio, a criminal civil rights lawyer, used to quote poetry in his final arguments. In our modern days, our poets are not just the Beatles and the Beach Boys, but also Jay-Z, Common, Snoop Dog, and Eminem. I suggest listening to these hip-hop artists to gain insight into the collective unconscious of our younger jurors.

Is there anything we can do after the final argument, other than explain to the jury what to do under certain circumstances? Yes, even though we cannot go into the jury room, we can continue to be close—physically, emotionally, and spiritually—by maintaining *presence*.

There is one very powerful way to continue your presence: by being at the courthouse *at all times* when the jurors are deliberating, from early in the morning when they arrive until the last juror has left for the day.

You need to be available when questions are asked and seen when a juror goes out to make a cell phone call or smoke a cigarette. If you are not there to be seen, the jurors may discount your commitment.

Furthermore, your client must be with you at all times. The jurors need to be thinking about you and the client. You must continue to show that same unity and family transference that the jury has projected on you during the trial.

By understanding these psychodynamics and combining this understanding with trial skills and methods taught by our modern trial masters, our presentation will be that much richer. We will have communicated the deeper perspective affecting inner awareness and intuition, which fosters the power to persuade.

PART IV

Using
Emerging Principles
From Other Fields

Chapter 27

Medicine

As trial lawyers, we must continue to monitor other professions and fields of study, as well as our own. We always have to be aware that jurors are somewhat skeptical of us and our integrity and motives, having been bombarded by insurance and institutional advertising against us for many years.

What we also need to consider is the concurrent siege of propaganda against doctors for medical errors, the questions raised by the health care bill about the mandatory electronic charting rules and accuracy of record-keeping, and the increasing use of the Internet by patients to self-diagnose and check doctors' recommendations.

If doctors are our natural enemies, then they are also our closest allies. What we want is to have our medical experts help us with their perceived trustworthiness, but at the same time use our jurors' disappointment with their own medical experiences to lead them to rule against the doctors on the other side. As a common one-liner goes, "There are doctors who graduated at the top of the class, but there are also those who were at the bottom." We need to make our experts the top of the class and the defense experts the bottom dwellers. The "what questions" discussed earlier can help with this.

In one case, through Internet research I found that the doctor we were suing had been sued five other times over a three-year period. Further research showed that the doctor's wife had been in rehab for several drunk-driving violations. While the judge wouldn't let us introduce these facts directly, we were able to create an inference that this doctor had personal problems around the time of the negligent surgery.

In medicine, great thinkers like Atul Gawande, M.D., and Jeremy Groopman, M.D., play the same role in advancing better quality in patient care as Ball, Keenan, and others have played in making us better trial lawyers. Furthermore, many of their tools and techniques designed to help doctors improve performance can be used by trial lawyers as well.

Gawande is a Boston surgeon and writer. His books and numerous articles, primarily in *The New Yorker* magazine, focus on how to reduce medical errors and address a variety of related topics, including the economics of medicine, the effect of apology on medical malpractice suits, and most recently, how a simple tool set of standardized checklists—similar to that of airline pilots—can substantially lower medical errors.

We can borrow from Gawande in the same way Ball and Keenan have borrowed from sociologists to formulate the "reptile" theory—and in the way I have borrowed from Freud and other psychologists here in the use of methods to influence the unconscious.

For example, Gawande has shown that apology is a powerful deterrent to medical malpractice lawsuits. Can we use apology to increase our chances of winning jury trials? Should we have our clients apologize for suing, telling the jury that they are "not the kind of person who sues" and then explaining why they decided to sue in this particular case? Would it be wise to apologize for asking the jury to redistribute wealth and create an entitlement? Should we stand up and directly apologize for a plaintiff's bad baggage, while still asking the jury for damages to be paid by an otherwise exemplary defendant?

I think there is much to be gained by trying this out in the courtroom. First, however, we need to conduct focus groups on this counterintuitive strategy of apology.

Gawande's method for reducing medical errors by using checklists for medical procedures is likewise worth a consideration. Many of us already use checklists in one way or another, but it is instructive to know that they have been shown to substantially reduce error in other fields. We also need to minimize mistakes and omissions in the courtroom.

Errors can adversely affect our positive transference with jurors by negating our transparency and genuineness. Hence, a short checklist of, for example, every topic we want to cover with each witness would be a great way to reduce our own blunders and increase our alliance with the jury.

If the major problem we face is asking a jury to take money from defendant A and give it to plaintiff B, we may be able to use the methods that doctors increasingly use to prevent errors and, thereby, avoid liability.

Chapter 28

Politics

The political divide is very deep and wide. We are in a stalemate between Democrats and Republicans, liberals and conservatives. One of the biggest issues is redistribution of wealth through taxation. I have addressed the "Peter and Paul" problem earlier, which is the lawyer's equivalent of this issue.

The Republican Party has made tort reform and frivolous lawsuits part of its platform and agenda. I think this is a bigger impediment to a fair jury trial than we might think.

Barack Obama was elected president by a wide margin in 2008, but quickly became a divisive figure, hated by many who feared redistribution of wealth through taxation. With a Democratic majority in Congress, several highly controversial bills were passed. Those bills, most prominently "Obamacare," are both expensive and seen by many as attempts to transfer the wealth of hardworking people to the less hardworking ones.[38]

Since societal benefits of universal health insurance and better education are widely acknowledged, conservatives were initially expected to compromise and work with Obama and the Democratic majority to increase federal input into health care and education policy. Increased federal taxation on the wealthy was deemed inevitable to pay for the expansion of federal power, and the fact that only a very small minority would suffer increased income tax was seen as the Democrats' ace in the hole.

38 Taxing the wealthy to reduce the deficit is a popular concept, but "wealthy" has not yet been defined. At least 50% of people do not want any more taxes on anyone if the money is going to be transferred to those seen as undeserving (e.g., the willingly unemployed, unwed mothers, welfare babies). It is unclear if these 50% are even willing to transfer wealth to the innocent (e.g., the sick, the fired, the injured). This is our "Peter and Paul" problem.

But a curious thing happened. The leaders of the Republican Party like Sen. Mitch McConnell and Sen. Jim DeMint, as well as young House leaders like Rep. John Boehner and Rep. Paul Ryan, refused to collaborate or even compromise with the majority, encouraging a grassroots uprising of a group that called itself the Tea Party. They claimed that Obama was a socialist and a liar and only wanted to redistribute (take) our money and give it to the poor, who were lazy and refused to work. They thus pushed the envelope to the most extreme position possible—in effect, polarizing the issue.

Fox News and its popular hosts like Bill O'Reilly and Sean Hannity, as well as radio hosts like Rush Limbaugh, all over the country decried Obama's agenda as the ruination of America and American exceptionalism. The liberal and educated press ridiculed the seemingly cruel and selfish Tea Party members, and pundits again predicted the end of the Republican Party and an era of Democratic rule.

The Republican Party was characterized as the "Party of No." Its leaders publicly refused to agree to any new legislation and used parliamentary rules like the filibuster to keep any legislation they opposed from even making it to the floor for a vote. They voted "no" as a unified block and refused to even meet with the Democratic leaders.

Pundits predicted disaster for these conservative tactics, but they were wrong. By the 2010 election, Republicans and their grassroots allies, the Tea Partiers, had the country in an uproar, refusing to compromise even a little bit. However, they won the midterm elections, in a landslide, taking over the majority in the House and cutting the Democratic majority in the Senate to a slim margin.

Notably, this political battle is still raging today, even within the Republican Party. Some Republicans like Sen. Rand Paul advocate doing away with all entitlements, agencies, and even the income tax. "Entitlement" has become a dirty word, even though individual programs like Social Security and Medicare, which make up the rubric of entitlements, remain popular.

So, what can we as trial lawyers learn from all of this? How can we use it to our benefit? If we allow our trial to be one over whether our client is *entitled* to the defendant's money because of her injury, we will immediately lose at least half of the jurors. The challenge is to hold on to our empathetic jurors—those who will see the case as one of compensation—and at the same time get around the others' resistance to "tax" the defendant, no matter how fair it may seem.

We must explain how the legal system works and what principles allow us to "rob" Peter to pay Paul. We should polarize and make the jury force the other side to prove by a preponderance of evidence the unprovable: that our client is a bad person, a liar, and a thief.

We need to use therapeutic methods, jury science, and methods from other disciplines in a positive and professional manner. But also, we have to understand that the jury will give great credence to our unshakable, principled refusals to compromise—that there is great power in stating a position clearly and unequivocally and sticking to it under all pressure and ridicule, if we believe it.

This is a signal of transference and intuitive thinking of the unconscious of the jury. Along with this transference of powerful positive feelings comes transference of our authority and others' fear of us, similar to that of children to parents. Children expect and need the parent to say no, to set limits, and to stand on principle. That is why Friedman's thesis of rules and polarizing the case has great appeal to the jurors who are looking consciously and unconsciously for clarity and leadership from us. We need to act unequivocally and without compromise on universal principles. Such a stand is attractive and appealing.

So, on matters of principle—including the principle that it is fair to order defendant A to pay plaintiff B to rectify injury—we need to directly tell the jurors that there is no compromise on this, that we will not equivocate on these issues, and that they should not either in deliberations. Transfer of wealth in this venue is part of the deal, part of the responsibility of all citizens. We should do what Obama has done and appeal to a sense of history and patriotism, *as well as* what McConnell, Boehner, and the Republicans have done—appeal to the sense of a principled stand.

Despite all of this battling and line drawing, there is also an unconscious need to compromise. This is not really contradictory, but it is our responsibility as trial lawyers to satisfy these seemingly inconsistent unconscious desires by approving of both. We can do this by refusing to compromise on the principle, but allowing some compromise on the details. Remember how old-school attorney Ed Rood used his damages chart? The chart assumed there were damages, without equivocation, but allowed a range for juror consideration.

In all issues during the trial, we must use transference to communicate to the jurors our unshakeable belief in our case in all ways. Polarizing, as recommended by Friedman, is one way of doing this. But in order to polarize effectively, we must first establish a positive transference and create an atmosphere of trust, so jurors feel comfortable in accepting our position that the defense position is extreme and must be rejected.

No matter how we feel about Obama, the Tea Party, or the "Party of No," we owe a great debt to the recent political struggle, which has shown us how the collective unconscious permeates and influences large groups. We can use these very strategies to encourage principled stands by jurors in deliberations. We should ask jurors in our final argument not to give in to attempts to compromise on causation and liability, but only on the amount.

A lot of trials are lost when jurors find the defendant negligent but not causative. Many times this is the result of compromise. We cannot allow this to happen, as such a verdict is not a partial win for us—it is a total loss.

Chapter 29

News Media

Concurrent with our extreme political adversity is the rising phenomenon of how news is received in modern America via both cable television and the Internet. Very few of us get our news from only one source nowadays. We no longer have a shared and trusted channel like *CBS Evening News* with Walter Cronkite.

News is delivered and received in sound bites, through videos on YouTube, and via social networks like Facebook and Twitter. However, the most important source of news these days by far is cable television, with programs like *Fox News*, *The Daily Show*, and *The Colbert Report* on Comedy Central. Of course, online publications like the *Drudge Report* and *The Huffington Post* also play a significant role.

Recent polls show that a plurality of Americans under 35 years of age consider Jon Stewart of *The Daily Show*, a comedian, to be the most watched and the most credible news source. The adversarial hosts on Fox cable network like Glenn Beck, Bill O'Reilly, and Sean Hannity are similarly popular suppliers of information for conservatives. Beck is a former rock-'n'-roll disc jockey, O'Reilly a former host of a network show about Hollywood, and Hannity a former radio DJ.

Stewart specializes in political humor, satire, and exposing hypocrisy. He focuses mostly on the hypocrisy of Republicans and conservatives, but will nail Democrats and liberals as well. One important tool that Stewart uses is showing video clips of inconsistent statements made by politicians and other leaders. Stewart then lightly mocks these lawmakers, while delivering the news. It appears obvious now that at least the younger people would rather have the news delivered this way than deadpan and "just the facts, ma'am."

We have already discussed how important technology is to younger jurors. Make sure you show videos or clips from the Internet. Definitions, jury instructions, rules, and the jury interrogatories must all be shown on boards or screens.

Humor and satire are also strategies that can be helpful to us in communicating facts and information to juries. I would recommend using humor and satire sparingly, though, unless it comes easily to you. Look for a way to expose hypocrisy in a lighthearted manner. The jury of cable TV watchers will "get it."

Obviously, humor has to be delivered just right or it can damage the case. If you don't feel comfortable, don't do it. The delivery should be very friendly, not cutting or mean, and you need to mug after the zinger to show the jury that you are just kidding. Humor can allow you to rise above the fray and get the jury comfortable with the idea of transferring wealth.

We should ask how each juror gets the news in voir dire. If it is from Fox, think about a peremptory. If from Stewart, find out more. The problem is that everyone is skeptical about government these days, and the courts are government. It may make sense to explain how cheap the courts are compared to other government agencies. We may also want to figure out a way to separate ourselves from politicians by talking about how we run a small business, make a payroll, and employ people.

Chapter 30

Sports

Our society and culture are dominated by sports, so sports analogies and metaphors are very familiar to most people.[39] Sports are uniquely similar to trials because both involve a central contest in which one side wins and the other one loses. It naturally follows that learning about emerging strategies for success in sports is useful to us as trial lawyers, since we also seek ways to beat the competition.

It may be truth or legend that Spence has never lost a jury trial, but the rest of us surely have. The big question is how we handle losing. How do we accept the bitter stone and gather the courage to try the next one? All of us know colleagues who never recovered from a big loss—financially, emotionally, or both. Some changed careers or specialties, and some simply settled everything, farmed out, or chose to co-counsel every case.

Some of us have stayed the course, but are embarrassed and justify our losses by blaming the judge, the jury, or even our clients. We rail against the opposing counsel for unfair tactics and against the judge for improper jury instructions.[40] This is okay, so long as internally we recognize our responsibility for losing, self-analyze our mistakes and weaknesses, and learn how to avoid them in the future.

In sports, losing is part of the game, an integral part of the experience. We will do best as trial lawyers if we can incorporate losing into our

39 Although some would say not to overuse sports analogies for fear of alienating female jurors, I disagree. In my view, women are simply interested in sports in a different way.

40 Although I believe that jury instructions can make a winning case a loser, we do not control this part of the trial, so we have to figure out a way to make the bad instructions favorable somehow. This is a unique skill that has not been well explored by our trial bars and associations.

experience in the same way as Tiger Woods and Roger Federer have done in recent years—humbled but unbowed. We can still be successful and brilliant trial lawyers and lose an occasional jury. What's important is that we learn from the experience to become ever wiser, ever more intuitive, and better.

Let's look at Rory McIlroy, the great young Northern Irish golfer. In the 2011 Masters, he was leading the field by five strokes early in the final round. He was cruising to his first major victory at 21 years of age. And then he dropped his guard. Still ahead by a stroke at the ninth hole, he hit balls into water, sand, and deep rough, missed easy putts, and gradually slipped down, scoring a 43 on the back nine and slipping out of the top 10.

Several months later, McIlroy began the U. S. Open at Congressional Club in Washington, D.C., with an opening-round 65. He never looked back, winning by eight strokes and setting 12 gold records along the way. He played brilliantly in the final round, hitting fairways and greens, making the most of his chances, and working out of trouble with a level head and strategic thinking.

In his interviews after the tournament, McIlroy made some points that we ought to incorporate into our experience as trial lawyers so that we, too, can come back to victory following a loss.

McIlroy said that he let the loss go after a few days and then started preparing for the next tournament. He realized that he had departed from his original planning for the Masters and tried to extend his lead. This led to mistakes, as he tried to hit shots he had not prepared for. He called Jack Nicklaus and asked for advice on how to finish. Nicklaus advised him to always shape his shots into the green from the bigger part of the green toward the pin, as this gives a greater margin for error and reduces the possibility of blow-up holes.

So, how do we incorporate some of this golf wisdom as we pick ourselves off the ground after a loss?

I recently lost a trial. The defense counsel surprised and sandbagged me by taking a seemingly unrelated statute into the case during the direct examination of the defendant, and the judge gave an erroneous jury instruction based on the statute.[41]

41 The case was settled in post-trial motions.

Here is what happened:

I prepared the case, my witnesses, and the experts to address the standard of care for an emergency room doctor when faced with a patient showing signs of severe emotional distress. We proved that the doctor had failed to use precautions to prevent harm to the patient, who had *voluntarily presented* herself to the emergency room, asking for help for severe depression and anxiety. We offered expert testimony that a standard psychiatric interview must include a question to rule out suicidal thoughts.

We presented hospital policies and security policies that should have been used to protect the patient's well-being and safety when the doctor abruptly left the room to take a phone call.

However, the defense—without prior notice—presented a state statute that defined the requirements for the *involuntary probate* of mentally ill persons by police officers or other law enforcement officials.

Since this statute addressed constitutional standards protecting the rights of a person who did not want to be hospitalized, it required findings by the court that the patient presented a serious risk of harm to herself or others. This statute was not for emergency room physicians caring for a patient, but for guiding detention determinations by judges after a full hearing. Thus, the defense was able to reframe the case as one of the constitutional right of a patient to be free from restraint and detention, rather than one of the safety of the patient.

My client's daughter—this poor, confused, and depressed young lady—had eloped from the hospital, being chased by a nurse, and jumped off a wall to her death. Our case was that a reasonably careful ER doctor should have thoroughly evaluated her for suicidal thoughts before leaving her alone in the room. Or, if he had not yet conducted an evaluation, he should have secured her with a guard outside the room or a nurse or aide in the room until his return.

We had pretty good evidence on this, but the statute raised another issue that resonated and played to the shared unconscious of the jury: the fear of being probated without probable cause. A trial lawyer has to be ever vigilant, as defense can present some "rules of the road," such as patient rights, that resonate with the jury and affect the outcome of the trial.

In every setback, we have to go beyond the actions of our opponents and the judge, examining our own reactions and lessons learned.

So, here is what I learned:

1. If defense counsel pulls a rabbit out of the hat, ask for a recess and take some time to think about how to respond. I didn't do that. I objected and tried to convince the judge to exclude the irrelevant material, but to no avail. Instead of objecting loudly and letting the jury think I was out maneuvered, I should have called a timeout, studied, planned, and come back to the courtroom with a plan.
2. During the timeout, file a written brief, even if only one or two pages, so the judge knows that this material is newly injected without notice, and that there is authority against it. Ask the judge for a limiting instruction if he rules against you.
3. Put on a rebuttal witness to tear down the defense's case on this new point. Have the last evidentiary word.
4. In the final argument, explain clearly and methodically why the new evidence and jury instruction favors your side.
5. Don't panic. I panicked and tried the rest of the trial on their terms. We ended up trying the case on a higher standard that we couldn't fulfill. I should have taken a day and re-prepared my cross-examinations of the experts to undermine the statute.

There are other lessons that we can incorporate from sports figures as well. One is from the world of tennis, where each player, like each lawyer in a trial, is alone in the contest.

Brad Gilbert is a former professional tennis player, coach, and commentator. While on the professional tennis circuit, he was regarded as a very smart player, but one with limited athletic skills compared to his top competitors. He wrote a book titled "Winning Ugly," in which he admitted his own weaknesses and fears, much like Spence has done in his books about jury trials. Gilbert advises watching and analyzing the dynamics of the opposing player to figure out his strengths, in order to then use these strengths as a weapon against him.[42]

Gilbert prepared for a match with a list of important things about his opponent. This is similar to the checklists that Gawande recommends to reduce medical errors. We should always maintain a list not only of the tasks to be performed at trial, but also of the weaknesses of the opposing lawyer and the case. By adapting preparation methods such as focus groups and checklists from other disciplines, we can gain a better understanding of our weaknesses and strengths, our opponents' weaknesses and strengths, and how to exploit them.

We also hear from world-class athletes how they engage in *visualization* before a game, actually fantasizing how they will score, run, or jump. This is similar to the therapeutic method of using fantasies and dreams to bring a patient to greater self-awareness. In the courtroom, we can engage in psychodrama and vivid descriptions, as well as telling the story in the present tense, to prompt jurors to visualize the surgery or accident in a more powerful way.

Finally, we have to recognize the emergence of instant replay in almost all sporting events as something that spectators now expect. We have to be prepared for a future where jurors will be able to replay the testimony of all witnesses on iPads or other modern gadgets. This will create a need for greater transparency by trial lawyers: no more shading the testimony of a prior week to minimize the damage of that witness or bolstering the testimony of our witnesses to make the case stronger.

Just as instant replay has changed sports, it will surely change the way we argue our cases in the final argument.

As always, genuineness, transparency, and empathy will be necessary to persuade juries to take the step of compensating our client with the defendant's money. But, we may now have to use more modern methods, learn more about technology, and recognize that jurors may well be accessing outside information to verify what they are learning in the courtroom. Thus, we will have to find a way to manage psychodynamics not only in the courtroom, but also outside.

---

42 B. Gilbert and S. Jamison. "Winning Ugly," Touchstone, 1994.

Chapter 31

Social Networking and Public Relations

I have a young friend who recently completed his MBA at Harvard. He is brilliant and wise beyond his years. I recently defended his father, a doctor, who had been wrongly accused of improprieties with patients. The jury acquitted him after a two-week trial. The son's superior social networking and computer researching skills helped me win the trial.

This young man assembled a group of friends, a freelance reporter and blogger, a medical researcher, and a public relations professional to assist me in my trial preparation, as well as during the trial. They mined the Internet for information about all aspects of the case, from the witnesses, to the trial history of the prosecutor, to the social networking of the jurors. We would all meet every morning before trial, and I would get reports from the group.

During the trial, the group set up a "war room" of laptop computers on the benches outside the courtroom and continuously mined the Internet for anything that was required. I probably used less than 1% of the information they had found, but that 1% was valuable, particularly in letting me know about the things I did not have the opportunity to ask in voir dire, such as that one of my jurors was a member of the Sierra Club and another had interest in liberal politics.

It is amazing how comforting it is to cross-examine witnesses and know where they live, what music they like, what their spouses and children do for a living, what interests they have, etc. Is this wrong to do? Is there any ethical problem with this? I grappled with this at first, but finally decided that I have as much right to read information in the public domain as a witness has to visit my website or Facebook page and learn about me before taking the stand.

Make no mistake, this type of knowledge will change law and trial procedures. Social networking and online mining are just beginning. Soon, we will be able to find out every life detail of every participant in the trial. Is this good? I don't know, but it is reality.

In addition to catering to my requests, the group tracked stories about the case in the local newspaper, on the Internet, and in other media. Jurors are not sequestered, and although the judge tells them not to read the paper or watch the news, common sense and experience tell us that at least one or several of them are investigating on their own. The group informed me as to what was in the media each day, and I tried to figure out a way to fit it into my presentation. I was not able to use very much of this information, but what I learned made me more comfortable. Knowledge is power, indeed!

The group also came up with a brilliant idea of pitching stories that had positive relevance to our case to reporters, bloggers, and radio and TV hosts, hoping to have these stories run in the media during the trial. An example would be a positive story about psychiatrists in general or about a psychiatric issue. We were not successful in this endeavor, but it is worth trying.

My young friend has now incorporated a company offering this service, which he calls "strategic trial consulting." This company will use strategies to reach the unconscious of the jurors outside the courtroom. Part of the effort is to mine information in the public domain about the jurors to increase the trial lawyer's knowledge about each juror. Unlike the therapist, who has months or years to gather information about the patient from the patient herself, the trial lawyer has only minutes to find out about the juror, and little more about other witnesses beyond deposition testimony.

Information is the lifeblood of influence. The more we know about the jurors, the witnesses, the opposing counsel, and even the judge, the better we can do in using our trials skills and such methods as transference and projection to succeed in the courtroom.

Chapter 32

Neuroscience

The advance of neuroscience is a big thing for trial lawyers. Knowledge is quickly expanding in this area, with plenty of research funding from government and private enterprises, foundations, and nonprofits.

Trial lawyers must keep abreast of advances in the understanding of how the brain works at the cellular level. While this field is still in its infancy, much has already been learned about the functioning of the brain. A comprehensive digest of the research on this topic is beyond the scope of this book, but trial lawyers must be aware that ultimately this knowledge will be at least as important as the theoretical work of Freud and Jung in learning about the unconscious and all of its mysteries.

One outstanding work in this burgeoning field relevant to trial lawyers is "How We Decide," by Jonah Lehrer.[43] Lehrer looks at the history of the study of the brain and comes to some valuable conclusions as to how the brain organizes complex information and adds emotional content, leading to decision-making.

One of Lehrer's main hypotheses is that the pre-frontal cortex of the brain is the "referee" of thinking. Lehrer submits that in this part of the brain, the powerful emotional thought process (the unconscious) is filtered and controlled by the rational thought process emanating from the frontal cortex. The frontal and pre-frontal cortexes are the last parts of the brain to mature, sometimes as late as teenage years. This suggests that the process for decision-making may be more involved than other brain functions. This understanding may help us during final argument and explains why subtlety is so effective.

43 Lehrer has been disgraced by his admission of plagiarism in some articles for The New Yorker. Nonetheless, as a gatherer of new research and thinking, he has important information for trial lawyers.

Historically, the brain was studied through observation of tissues and activity during open surgery. More recently, however, scientists have been able to map brain activity via radiographic MRI studies. For example, through such studies, tumors and other lesions in the frontal region of the brain have been shown to cause a reduction in rational thought. Lehrer suggests that MRI studies can also be used to confirm or challenge results of decision-making studies conducted purely through psychological testing. Much is expected to be learned in this area in the next few years.

Lehrer cites the famous "marshmallow" study conducted by Walter Mischel of Stanford University, which determined that 4-year-old children who were able to defer a basic need for gratification based on a promise of greater gratification at a later time eventually became more successful adults.[44] Through questions in voir dire about deferral of gratification, we may find out which jurors will require framing and immediate answers and which ones will allow us to use hinting and intuition to put our case together.

In some cases with more complex liability issues, we might prefer "deferred gratification" jurors, who will be more patient and allow us more time to show causation. In other cases, where the issue of liability is clearer and the amount of damages is the primary contest, we may prefer "instant gratification" jurors.

Lehrer also touts the work of George Miller, a psychologist who tested the number of data the average person can process and remember, publishing the findings in "The Magical Number Seven, Plus or Minus Two."[45] A collateral study determined that if subjects were given important data in conjunction with irrelevant data, but told that the irrelevant data was important, the brain could not easily dismiss the irrelevant data. Miller called this the "anchoring effect." This finding can help us decide how to best present information during the trial and in the final argument.

---

44 W. Mischel, E. B. Ebbeson, and A. R. Zeiss. "Cognitive and Attentional Mechanisms in Delay of Gratification," Journal of Personality and Social Psychology, 21(2), 204–218, 1972.

45 G. A. Miller. "The Magical Number Seven, Plus or Minus Two: Some Limits on Our Capacity for Processing Information," Psychological Review, 63, 81–97, 1956.

Probably the most valuable study cited by Lehrer for trial lawyers is the MIT study on the effect of providing more or less information to subjects involved in a stock market investing game. In this study, one group was given only the daily price increase or decrease of certain stocks. The other group was given a steady stream of data about each stock, in addition to the price information. The result? The group with *less* information performed significantly better in deciding how to invest. This suggests that we can use less information, relying instead on the jury's intuition and subtlety in the final thrust.

As Lehrer says, "We know a lot more than we know that we know." This simple concept certainly applies to jurors, both individually and as a group. If we have properly directed the jury's unconscious throughout the trial, the information they have gained will allow them to make decisions in conjunction with what they already knew coming into the courtroom. Studies of the frontal and pre-frontal cortexes teach that we have to respect this when we deliver the final argument.

The fact is, other than arming the jurors on our side with a review of the important documents we want them to use to persuade the other jurors, as well as displaying important portions of the jury instructions and a chart with damages calculations for the jury interrogatory forms, the final argument may well be superfluous.

I remember Paul Newman in the movie "The Verdict" standing up and telling the jury: "You know what to do. Do the right thing." How would a jury react to that? From my discussions with jurors and thousands of hours in the courtroom in front of juries, I think they would react very well. One day I may try it.

PART V

Merging Trial Strategy & Dynamic Psychology To Overcome Challenges

Chapter 33

Women Trial Lawyers—Using Gender as an Advantage

One of the biggest changes in law that I have seen in my 30-some years as a trial lawyer is the huge advance of women in the profession. While we still have a small minority in our trial associations, there are many more female defense attorneys. The psychological impact a woman has on a jury as either a judge or a lawyer is quite profound. Women lawyers must recognize that there are advantages and disadvantages in the unconscious way they are received by the jury. They need to capitalize on their unique strengths and minimize the damage that can be done if they show weakness or fear.

I have practiced before many female judges and have had at least three major trials against lead women lawyers on the other side. One of these lawyers has represented hospitals and doctors for years. She is, without a doubt, the finest courtroom defense counsel I have ever seen, regardless of gender. K is tall, red-headed, attractive, and plain-spoken. There is little girlishness in her, but she is feminine nonetheless.

What K does at the unconscious level is embody the big sister that everyone would love to have. She is smart without apology, bossy without being overbearing, and cynical and sarcastic without being obnoxious. She is unfailingly polite, and when she skewers a witness—for example, an expert doctor on the plaintiff's side—the witness doesn't realize he has been scalped until he is sitting on the airplane on the way home hours later. But the jury knows.

When it comes to argument, K is exceedingly brief and to the point. She doesn't waste time with platitudes. She might throw in a little criticism of the plaintiff lawyer just to show that she is not intimidated, but mostly she just stands in front of the jury and talks to them. K uses humor and sarcasm as a tool to create positive transference. Her humor is often self-deprecating and subtle. She directs the jury to one or two key documents, tells the jury why she won, and sits down.

With her brevity, femininity, focus, and matter-of-fact style, she reaches the unconscious of the jury in a way that would be unusual for male plaintiff attorneys to do.

I foresee that women lawyers will become more and more prominent in years to come. The great advantage that they have going into trial is the universal unconscious feeling of respect and trust for the maternal role in our society. In our unconscious minds, women nurture and care for us, sacrifice their own pleasure for the family, and have great integrity and trustworthiness.

On the other side of the coin, the worst female lawyer I have ever seen in the courtroom was J, an employment defense attorney with a large and prestigious firm. J was smart and attractive, but had none of the other winning qualities that allowed K success in the courtroom. J was demanding, got hysterically loud and abrasive if things didn't go her way, and was accusatory and belittling toward opposing counsel and plaintiff witnesses. She was not satisfied to make points in a matter-of-fact manner; she was theatrical and explosive. Needless to say, she was not well suited for the courtroom and had a short career as a trial lawyer.

Age is another factor that a trial lawyer must use effectively to maximize the psychodynamic advantage. A young lawyer will have a far different type of transference with jurors than an older one with gray hair. The young lawyer will evoke a more childish transference, and the older lawyer a more parental one. It is important to think about this when you approach the jury. Put simply, a trial lawyer ought to act his or her age, either with the vigor and enthusiasm of youth or the wise and patient generosity of the aged.

Gender and age are important factors for evaluating jurors as well. The common belief is that female jurors are more plaintiff-oriented, but harder on female plaintiffs. Older jurors are thought to be stingy with damages. It is critical to talk to jurors about these stereotypes. There should not be any problem with telling them about these stereotypes and asking whether they might fit into a particular one, so long as it is done empathetically and with unconditional positive regard.

Chapter 34

Arguing Equity

The largest problem I see in applying psychodynamic principles successfully is the obtuse and ambiguous jury instructions of law. Smart defense lawyers who know that the jury's unconscious has been powerfully influenced by the plaintiff lawyer's psychodynamic positivity, genuineness, and transparency wait patiently for the judge to instruct the jury at the end of the trial. There is just nothing worse for the plaintiff trial lawyer than the judge droning on and on about all of the reasons the jury cannot find for the plaintiff.

Many parts of the jury instructions are so confusing and limiting that the judge in effect ends up telling the jury, "Sorry, I know you like the plaintiff and his lawyer and feel very empathetic toward them, but I have to tell you that the law does not allow you to award damages unless they have jumped over tall buildings in a single bound, were faster than a speeding bullet, etc."

Unfortunately, we are stuck with the jury instructions of law. The instructions on the burden of proof, proximate cause, and damages make it close to impossible to win a case for the plaintiff if these instructions are applied strictly by the jury. So, what can we do? The answer is to merge what we know about psychotherapeutic principles and trial strategies to frame the most troubling jury instructions in a winning perspective in the final argument.

The instruction on the burden of proof is a prime example. A shrewd defense lawyer may tell a jury that the judge will instruct them that the plaintiff has the burden, the defendant has no burden, and if there is a tie, the defendant would win. The word "burden" is so heavily freighted, it almost sounds like the plaintiff is being called a burden.

The defense lawyer would then accurately recite the "no sympathy" instruction and inform the jury that as much as they might like to award the plaintiff some money, they can't because the law doesn't allow it.

We must understand the unconscious power of this argument and fight back against this tactic. The way to do it is to learn what I call the "equity instructions" and highlight them to the jury in the rebuttal final argument.

In law school, we have learned that there is *equity* and *law*—equity being non-monetary remedies and law representing the damages. Jurors are totally unfamiliar with this dichotomy. Yet, this dichotomy, I believe, can be our ace in the hole in a playing field that is tilted against us.

The most crucial equity instruction is the one addressed earlier in this book, which explains that the defendant also has a burden—the burden to support what he claims with evidence. In Ohio, the jury instruction on burden of proof states, "The person who claims certain facts exist must prove them by a preponderance of evidence." Other states have similar instructions. My recommendation is that you must put this part of the burden instruction on a screen in the rebuttal final argument.

This then leads us to another equity instruction that is clearly favorable to our side. It is the jury instruction that states, "Your duty as a juror is to arrive at a fair and just verdict." This instruction in Ohio is given during the court's closing remarks, after the substantive instructions.

We need to focus on how the jury receives these equity instructions not only individually, but as a collective unconscious. The group needs to know that there is a justification to go beyond the complexity of "preponderance of evidence" and "proximate cause," those unfamiliar and difficult concepts that can interfere with the group's decision-making; that the defendant has a burden, too; and that not just inelastic concepts like the "standard of care" or "proximate cause" but fairness is at stake.

Thus, we need to tell the jury that the primary task is not law but *equity*, and that they are being instructed to find the truth, come up with a fair verdict, and apply justice. In this way, we can urge the jurors to do their duty that the judge has instructed them to do. We should tell them to "look at the big picture"; this is a good one-liner for the rebuttal portion of the final argument.

"Equity" equals "fairness" in the minds of most people. This is what we want. Ball and Keenan postulate in the "reptile" theory that this larger context is really about the safety of the community. By setting rules and showing how they apply not only to the case at hand but also to the larger scope that affects each juror, we give jurors the power to rule for the plaintiff in the name of self-preservation. This, too, is an equitable argument.

Whether we accept the "reptile" concept of capitalizing on the common fears of the jury or other ways of submitting fairness and equity to the jury, what we all must realize is that jurors are both individuals and part of a group. An argument could be made that we appeal not to the "reptile," but to the successful operation of the group itself in accomplishing its sworn duty.

However, we must understand that there are biological bases of human thought, group dynamics, and psychology involved. A tremendous body of work exists that we can utilize in recognizing the powerful unconscious elements of these forces. The more we understand these biological bases for memory, intuition, and decision-making, the better we will be at persuasion, which is the ultimate and primary task of the trial lawyer.

Chapter 35

Getting the Verdict

Now that we have learned some basic information about the unconscious, transference and resistance, groups and intuition, and concurrent fields such as neuroscience and sports, the obvious question is: How do we translate this knowledge to a successful verdict?

Wilfred Bion, the father of group dynamics, described how extremely effective critical thinking is created in groups when we can merge the Beta (unconscious) elements of thought with the Alpha (conscious) elements of thought. A jury may have an intuition that the plaintiff is entitled to a favorable verdict at the end of the trial, but there may still be reluctance to give the defendant's money to the plaintiff. Of course, a lot of jurors will be aware that there is insurance, but in this age of panic about the cost of insurance, we cannot rely on this knowledge to blunt the effect of redistribution of wealth.

We can begin to overcome this potential obstacle by incorporating all of the things we have discussed in this book into our trial strategy, from the moment the jurors enter the courtroom till the time they leave to deliberate as a group. Our unconditional positive regard for the jurors, the witnesses on our side, and the judge will allow the jury to have esteem for us and give us room to make our arguments.

We should ask our jurors to have the same unconditional positive regard for the opposing or undecided jurors from voir dire throughout the trial. Our honesty should allow us to discuss openly the issue of transferring wealth. At the same time, we will be able to arm our jurors to convince the others that we are deserving of a favorable verdict.

The judge instructs jurors that they must come to a decision individually, but only after discussing, consulting, and deliberating with fellow jurors. This leads to the formation of a certain type of group. If we know there has been pairing, for example, which we know to be a very powerful force in group decision-making, we can appeal to the pair to persuade the others.

The members of the pair may ultimately disagree, however, which can really screw up our careful arguments. Juror Gail described how pairing had resulted in a surprising fallout in her case. The woman she had bonded with, eaten lunch with every day, and even discussed family matters with turned out to be on the opposite side once they entered the jury room for deliberations. Gail favored a plaintiff verdict, while her friend favored a defense verdict. Why? Gail felt that once the case was proven, it didn't matter where the money came from. The jurors had discussed and agreed that there was insurance, she recalled.

Shortly after entering the jury room and looking at the exhibits, some of the jurors wanted to ask the judge several questions—specifically, whether they could have the life care plans brought back for another review of the dollar amounts the lawyers had talked about in closing. Some of the other jurors wanted to come to a dollar amount quickly and leave; they felt trapped. Several also agreed with the defense; they were either willing to give nothing or only a small amount.

The jury went back to the basic liability and causation issue and discussed that thoroughly. Once liability against the defendant was the prevailing view of the majority, the argument shifted to amounts. Some jurors thought it was enough to award the injured man the amount under the life care plan and for pain and suffering, but others thought the wife should also get some money because she had so much responsibility. This became a huge sticking point.

The big issue was how much to give to the wife, who had to take care of her quadriplegic husband for the rest of their lives. The life care plan included $1 million for her needs. Gail's friend ridiculed the plan, stating, "And what about a million dollars for the wife's weekly manicures for the rest of her life?" Gail was shocked by this attitude from someone she had felt aligned with earlier.

While there was not a great amount of discussion about the lawyers and the parties, Gail felt that the unity of the plaintiff couple, as well as the unity between them and their lawyers, showed their credibility in asking for a large damage award. Clearly, the unconscious empathy of the jurors from the very first day of the trial was still alive in the jury room.

The thought Gail had about the defense was, "Who are they to decide what the plaintiffs will need to live?" From this thought, we can infer with some assurance that the defense did not create a positive transferential alliance with the jurors, or at least with the jurors who ultimately carried the day. We can also see that the more we can convince the jury to focus on the injured person and his needs, and not the fact that the money to pay for those needs would come from the other party, the better off we will be.

In the end, Gail reported, there was a general sentiment that the plaintiffs should win, even though the jurors were well aware that the proof put forth by the plaintiff side did not completely fulfill the judge's stringent instruction on what was needed to show causation, as no one could say for sure that earlier intervention would have changed the outcome. The best that could be said was that the doctor had not given the plaintiff a chance to get better by immediately taking action. The actual instruction was ignored by the jury, or at least modified to allow a verdict.

We have to remember how complex and confusing the jury instructions can be. What I have learned from Gail is that we can persuade the jury to ignore or modify adverse jury instructions. It may well be that in today's climate, we must convince them to do so. Jury nullification is here to stay. We must use it.

Chapter 36

Ethics

Recently, I had brunch with some old friends in Los Angeles who have been hugely successful in the entertainment field and are now active in an institute supporting the work of neuroscientists at UCLA. Having a long-standing interest in trials, these friends, husband and wife, have often discussed my cases with me. In a sense, they have been part of a circle I use as ad-hoc, mini focus groups when I get ready for trial.

During this get-together, we discussed some of the ideas presented in this book, as well as some of my experiences of using such methods as transference and intuition in jury trials to influence jurors' memory and decision-making.

One of my friends was concerned that I was possibly crossing a boundary from smart, intellectual lawyering to manipulation. We discussed this issue for some time. Some of the people at the table agreed that there was a degree of manipulation involved. Others felt either that there was no real manipulation or that it was okay, so long as the tactics were fair and honest.

The fact is, manipulation of many varieties does occur in all jury trials. It would be disingenuous to deny it. The fact that civil trials are in the end about money complicates things further. Money itself is a complex topic that many people have emotional difficulties discussing. Some people are so tied up in knots about money that they cannot concentrate on a tort trial. Trial lawyers have to learn about these types of deeply seated unconscious thoughts or risk doing a disservice to their clients and jurors.

The more we learn about the human brain, memory, psychology, and neuroscience, the better we can act to persuade jurors. Is this bad? Is this type of manipulation dishonest? Does it result in a societal wrong? If I know a lot about neuroscience and my opponent doesn't, is this an unfair advantage that skews justice?

These are legitimate questions. The question of how much influence the skill and knowledge of a lawyer can have over the outcome of a jury trial has long been debated in our field. Certainly, a trial lawyer who has studied and is purposely using psychological methods like transference may well gain more power over the jurors than one who does not understand this dynamic and its power.

The issue in a larger sense is trust. Whatever we as trial lawyers do in a trial, we cannot be successful if we give the jury a reason to distrust us. Attempts to maliciously or dishonestly manipulate the jury could well backfire, as the jury would experience transference in a negative way and gain intuition about the lawyer—and, therefore, his client—that could defeat an otherwise winnable case.

However, there is little doubt that a trial lawyer who is prepared, knows and cares about his client, has experience and skill, and integrates the tremendous power of the methods used by therapists and the principles of the unconscious will succeed with jurors. I don't see this as unethical or manipulative.

Chapter 37

Self-Analysis and Introspection

We can read about transference, group dynamics, and intuition, but how do we become skilled at these unconscious communications? How do we open ourselves up enough so that we can actually have unconditional positive regard for others?

I believe introspection is a key for any trial lawyer who wants to succeed. We need time alone, to allow us a painful reckoning with the past and our early childhood memories, especially before our trials. We need to be sensitive to the thoughts and feelings of others. Certainly, many trial lawyers are analytic patients and work on deep self-awareness.

Freud's first analytic patient was himself. He explored his powerful memories, trying to pull them out through fantasy and dreams, as well as deeper thought. Clearly, an awareness of our own unconscious is central to our ability to open up and influence the unconscious of jurors. This is one of our core responsibilities to our clients, because our only goal, really, is to get money for them to help them for the rest of their lives. Being self-aware and aware of the unconscious of the jury can help us reach this goal.

Freud, Jung, and the other scholars of the mind engaged in self-analysis as a means to better themselves as therapists. We can, and should, do this as well. It involves brutal honesty and thoughtfulness. It involves our own memories and fantasies, along with trying to discover the essence of our character and personality.

In the courtroom, no matter how many assistants we have, we trial lawyers are alone before the jury, as we have been alone at the counsel table, alone with our responsibility, and alone in our unconscious. How do we conquer this aloneness? How do we use it to help our clients? A trial lawyer cannot fear this aloneness, but should instead use it to become more sensitive to the loneliness of the jurors, as they sit in the jury box, silent and trapped, day after day.

Therapists are also alone with their patients, but they go through years of training in how to be comfortable in this role. In order to become certified as psychoanalysts, all psychiatrists and psychologists have to undergo their own analysis for a number of years. The thought is that only by learning about one's own unconscious can one competently analyze that of others. We trial lawyers have no similar training into ourselves and our minds, so we have to become self-aware by introspection.

A lawyer who has a firm sense of self, who has achieved the mature stage of life that Erik Erikson described as "identity over isolation,"[46] will be more likely to succeed with a jury—just as a therapist with a firm identity will surely have more success with a patient.

We can better understand what positive transference feels like by recreating in ourselves those feelings and emotions we felt as children. We need to remember what it felt like sitting in our pajamas on our father's lap on a Sunday morning, safely listening to him read the comics, or peacefully lying in bed with the smell of breakfast permeating from the kitchen. Can we feel the way we felt as fathers or mothers when our children were infants, cradled in our arms, drowsy and drifting to sleep as they suckled on a bottle?

It is this type of feeling that we want to convey to the jury—a feeling of safety and love, even in aloneness. We have to project this kind of warmth and positive caring to the jurors, making them feel less trapped and more committed. If we can get this type of feeling in ourselves in the courtroom, we can convey it to the jury, individually and as a group.

We can rely on our education in law, experience, and ongoing learning on the job and in the seminars. We can read books by great scholars of law and learn from other disciplines as well. However, the most important thing for the lonely trial lawyer is to be the positive unconscious force in the courtroom—transparent and genuine, as suggested by Carl Rogers.

Jung's work on personality types and archetypes may help us as well. Jung separated personality into two types: extroverts and introverts. Whether this formulation is strictly true or overly simplistic, it is criti-

46 E. Erickson. "Identity: Youth and Crisis," W. W. Norton & Company, 1968.

cally important that you recognize your type and act accordingly in the courtroom. An introvert's attempt to act in an extroverted manner will likely appear forced and strained.

Of course, we can never completely know ourselves and our unconscious motivations, needs, and desires. However, the more we understand that these unconscious thoughts and feelings exist deep inside, the better we can be at such things as transference and intuition, and the better we can transfer our own perceptions to the jurors.

If we operate best from feelings, rather than logic, that is the way to approach the jury. If we approach important decisions intuitively, rather than through our immediate sensory impressions, we need to approach the jury intuitively. The idea is to be genuine. We cannot be genuine unless we have good insight into ourselves.

Ultimately, the goal is to understand how the jury is receiving the information. Is this a jury we can approach with intuition, or do we have to load them with sensory perceptions through technology and demonstrations? The intuitive jury will "get it" more quickly and need less evidence. These are some of the things to consider as the trial proceeds.

In the end, we each need to decide what success means for us. What is the objective of our work in a given case, with a given jury, or with representing a certain client? What is the objective of our career? Is it to be the best we can be? Achieve million-dollar verdicts? Find the truth? Advance our reputation as trial lawyers?

It is good to think about this and come to grips with what you are looking for before you enter the courtroom, because that sense of self and narcissistic need will be on display and will be seen by the jury unconsciously. If the need is entirely narcissistic, or just for money for ourselves, we may not be the successful trial lawyer we seek to be.

In addition to success for your client, finding the truth, and fulfilling your need to succeed, the trial must also be about your commitment to the needs of the jurors, individually and as a group. Your ability to address these needs with subtlety and compassion is as much your role as putting medical records on the screen and showing the jury critical facts in an effective manner. The jury needs to win and succeed, too.

What I do, and what every trial lawyer ought to do before going into trial, is put away the files, the notes, and the notebooks, turn off the computer, and close the door. Think about who you are, where your life is and what you have achieved. At the same time, be positive and honest about what this trial means to you, your client, her family, and your family and staff. Think about the stake in the case for jurors, both as individuals and as a group representing the community.

Such self-analysis and self-reflection are important, because when you stand up and say, "Good morning, ladies and gentlemen," the jury is already processing you, already feeling the emotional stress of transference and beginning to gain an intuitive sense of the case, and already making important decisions.

Your inner identity and sense of self are at play in the courtroom. As much as you may try to use concepts and methods learned from reading Ball, Spence, and Keenan, your success in the trial depends on the way you use these methods, which in turn depends on the depth of your identity and self-awareness. If you have learned about yourself and have a firm inner core of identity, the jury will receive this as confidence.

You will also be able to stand in front of the jury box with greater ease and comfort if you know what the trial means to you and the jurors in front of you. By knowing yourself, recognizing your place and identity, and acting consistently with your core self throughout the trial, you will be able to give the jurors a sense of satisfaction and accomplishment in their decision-making process, solidifying your alliance once more before deliberations.

There is nothing in this world that can measure up to the experience of trying cases to juries. We are truly lucky and blessed in what we do. If you love the courtroom and can withstand the chaos and the mess, you can empower the jury by communicating and feeling what they feel and letting them come along on the journey. Then, when the jury comes back with the verdict you want, you can relax, knowing the job is complete and it was a job well done.

Acknowledgments

I am greatly indebted to the judges and lawyers who have taught me so much and mentored me in my career, such as Judges S. Arthur Spiegel, Bob Gorman, Tom Crush, Fred Cartolano, Bob Ruehlman, lawyers John Heilbrun, Gerry Spence, Professor Mariana Bettman, Dick Lawrence, Ann Lugbill, Chris Stegeman, Jim Chalfie, Ray Faller, Tom L. Conlan, Sr., and Jeff Harris, and even my worthy opponents like Walt Haggerty, Pat Dinkelacker, Mark Piepmeier, Karl Kadon, Mike Lyon, Ann Combs, Karen Carroll, and many, many others.

I want to thank all of the members of the Southwest Ohio Trial Lawyers Association for listening to me and advising me all of these years.

My father, Dr. Roy Whitman, my sister, Dr. Laura Whitman, and brother, Dr. Michael Whitman, psychoanalysts, psychologists, and scholars, guided me and helped me with my research. My sons, Jake and Andrew, listened and gave me ideas and constructive criticism. My wife, the awesome trial lawyer, Ginny Conlan Whitman, has made my life full and meaningful, has helped me every step of the way, and has made sure that I carefully think through what I write.

Trial consultants Mark Modlin and Becky Jones have trained me to see things not just as a lawyer, but as a friend to my clients. They have shown me the way in so many cases.

Finally, my assistants, Kathy Tucker and recently, Edward Greene, have looked after me and my clients, helped me succeed, and I could not have written this book without them.

Index

W

Y

About the Author

This book was written primarily in the Southern California Desert, a wonderful oasis and a quiet place to think and reflect. In the many trials Bruce B. Whitman has had over the years, he has dedicated himself to the success of his clients. He has many notable verdicts in both criminal defense and plaintiff tort cases. His verdicts and settlements in cases he has participated in over the past 33 years total in the many millions of dollars. He served as a Trustee for the Ohio Trial Lawyers Association from 2008-2011 and was a founding member of the Southwest Ohio Trial Lawyers Association. He is a leader in the Ohio trial bar in educating young lawyers in trial strategies and damages.

Made in the USA
Charleston, SC
26 May 2014